Vision of a Phoenix

VISION OF A PHOENIX
The Poems of Hŏ Nansŏrhŏn

*Translation with
Introduction and
Commentary by*

Yang Hi Choe-Wall

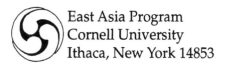

East Asia Program
Cornell University
Ithaca, New York 14853

The Cornell East Asia Series is published by the Cornell University East Asia Program (distinct from Cornell University Press). We publish affordably priced books on a variety of scholarly topics relating to East Asia as a service to the academic community and the general public. Standing orders, which provide for automatic billing and shipping of each title in the series upon publication, are accepted.

If after review by internal and external readers a manuscript is accepted for publication, it is published on the basis of camera-ready copy provided by the volume author. Each author is thus responsible for any necessary copyediting and for manuscript formatting. Address submission inquiries to CEAS Editorial Board, East Asia Program, Cornell University, Ithaca, New York 14853-7601.

The publication of this book was supported by a grant from the Korea Literature Translation Institute.

Number 117 in the Cornell East Asia Series
Copyright © 2003 by Yang Hi Choe-Wall. All rights reserved
ISSN 1050-2955
ISBN 1-885445-42-3 hc
ISBN 1-885445-17-2 pb
Library of Congress Control Number: 2003107103

20 19 18 17 16 15 14 13 12 11 10 09 08 07 06 03   9 8 7 6 5 4 3 2 1

Cover illustration: View of Mount Kumgang. Korean, Chosŏn period, 19th century. Album leaf; ink and colors on paper. Courtesy of Herbert F. Johnson Museum of Art, George and Mary Rockwell Collection, Cornell University. Cover design by Karen K. Smith.

For my children

Mikyung
and
Dai Kyu

Contents

Acknowledgements viii

Abbreviation ix

Editorial notes x

Introduction 1

Chapter I   Life of Hŏ Nansŏrhŏn 5

Chapter II The Sino-Korean Poetic Tradition
of the Late Sixteenth Century

Introduction 17

Confucian Literature of the early Chosŏn period 18

Move Towards Transition and the Three T'ang Talents of Korea 20

"Literature of the Outsiders": Away from Confucian Literature 23

Influence of *Hsien* Taoism on the Literature of the Outsiders 24

Shamanism as a Background for Korean *Hsien* Taoism 26

Chapter III Nansŏrhŏn's Writing

Part 1   Derivation of Text 30

Part 2   Study of Her Poetic Thought 33

Part 3   Nansŏrhŏn's Poetic Form 41

Part 4   Translations with Notes and Commentaries 44

Chapter IV Traditional Sources:
Translations, including discussion on the
issue of the authenticity of her work 102

Bibliography 119

Index 126

Table A   Traditional *akpu* titles found in Nansŏrhŏn's
collection and possible models for her *akpu* found in *YFSC* ..42

Table B   Arrangement of translated poems in the book 45

Acknowledgements

This book was written in the course of my work in the Division of Pacific and Asian History, in the Research School of Pacific and Asian Studies at the Australian National University, Canberra. The idea for it sprang from a piece of earlier research on Hŏ Nansŏrhŏn. It may, however, have remained as just an idea without the strong encouragement of two of my colleagues, Dr Kenneth Gardiner and Dr Andrew Fraser, who saw potential in my early notes for a book devoted to Hŏ Nansŏrhŏn's poetry. I am grateful, therefore, for their advice—given so freely whenever it was sought—as well as for their help in reading the manuscript and making many useful suggestions.

I owe a special acknowledgement to the Asian Collections of the National Library of Australia and the Australian National University Library. To the officers of these libraries I am much indebted for their help, always given so readily and courteously.

Abbreviations

CBYS	Yi Sugwang 李晬光, *Chibong yuŏl* 芝峰類說
CGTB	Kang Hyosŏk 姜斅錫, *Chŏn'go taebang* 典故大方
Ch.	Chinese
CTS	Ts'ao Yin 曹寅 et. al., ed., *Ch'üan T'ang shih* 全唐詩
CWS	Kuksa P'yŏnch'an Wiwŏnhoe ed., *Chosŏn wangjo shillok* 朝鮮王朝實錄
CYYMJ	Min Pyŏngdo 閔丙燾 ed., *Chosŏn yŏktae yŏryu munjip* 朝鮮歷代女流文集
DCM	E.T.C. Werner, *A Dictionary of Chinese Mythology*
HKCS	Hŏ Kyun 許筠, *Hŏ Kyun chŏnsŏ* 許筠全書
HGS	Kuksa P'yŏnch'an Wiwŏnhoe 國史編纂委員會 ed., *Han'guksa* 韓國史
HNCJ	Mun Kyŏnghyŏn 文暻鉉, tr. and ed., *Hŏ Nansŏrhŏn chŏnjip* 許蘭雪軒全集
KCSS	Hŏ Kyun, *Kukcho shisan* 國朝詩刪
KGT	*Kyŏngguk taejŏn* 經國大典. Korea (Republic). Pŏpchech'ŏ
Kor.	Korean
KRS	Chŏng Inji 鄭麟趾 et al., ed., *Koryŏsa* 高麗史
NSC	O Haein 吳海仁 ed., *Nansŏrhŏn shijip* 蘭雪軒詩集
SGSG	Kim Pushik 金富軾, *Samguk sagi*, 三國史記
SHML	Ch'a Chuhwan 車柱環, ed., *Shihwa wa mallok* 詩話와漫錄
TDYS	Chosŏn Kojŏn Kanhaenghoe, ed., *Taedong yasŭng* 大東野乘
tr.	Translated
YFSC	Kuo Mao-ch'ien 郭茂倩 ed., *Yüeh fu shih chi* 樂府詩集
YLSKS	Yi Kŭngik 李肯翊, *Yŏllyŏshil kisul* 燃藜室記述

Editorial Notes

In order to clarify the romanized Korean and Chinese words used in this book, the *han'gŭl* and the Chinese characters are given in the Index, and the English translation of the words within parentheses at their first appearance in the text. The romanization systems used for Korean and Chinese are the McCune-Reischauer Romanization System and the Wade-Giles Romanization System respectively. The works cited include, at their initial appearance in the text, an original description in Korean, Chinese or Japanese, as appropriate, together with the romanization. The bibliography is also presented in both the vernacular script and in romanized form.

Introduction

Among the outstanding literary figures of the Chosŏn Dynasty (1392-1910) perhaps the most imaginative was Hŏ Nansŏrhŏn (1563-1589), who lived and wrote her poetry during the reign of King Sŏnjo (r. 1567-1608), a period during which the Confucianization of society was a major factor. The inflexibility of the system and its concomitant sanctions placed severe restrictions on the lives of Korean women, particularly women of the *yangban* class (ruling class), to which Nansŏrhŏn, as one born into a celebrated family of high and distinguished lineage, belonged. As a girl, aided by both an eminent family tutor and by gifted brothers who were themselves later acclaimed as prominent writers, she showed an early aptitude for learning the Chinese classics. It was largely due to this encouragement that, in spite of the constraints of the system, she became not only one of the foremost poets but also a master calligrapher and painter. The Nansŏrhŏn of literary legend is a divinely gifted poet, possessed of unworldly qualities and enduring beauty, who predicted her own demise at the age of twenty-seven. The dearth of well-documented biographical material (with the exception of a few fragmentary descriptions of her life, gleaned from traditional sources) has no doubt contributed to the mystique that surrounds her.

The late sixteenth century is regarded as the Golden Age of *hanshi* (Sino-Korean poems). Of the literary works composed, *hanshi* made up the greater part and thus held pride of place as the principal genre of the time. Although undoubtedly of great importance to future Korean literature, *han'gŭl* (the Korean alphabet) received slow acceptance, being used initially to write so-called minor poetic genres, such as *shijo* or *kasa. Hanmun* (Korean writing in Chinese), on the other hand, persisted as the common means of literary expression of the time. This was largely due to the fact that Korea's social, political and educational systems were established in line with Chinese neo-

1

Confucian ideology and it was therefore natural for ideas and feelings to be expressed in *hanmun*, which the two countries had in common.

Of the various literary genres, poetry came to be the dominant form of literary expression. The reason for this can be traced back to the adoption of the T'ang system of government service examinations in 958 during the Koryŏ dynasty (918-1392). The most popular categories of examinations were the *chinsa* (Literary Licentiate) with emphasis upon *belles lettres* and *myŏnggyŏng* (the classics). Since the theoretical content made the study of the classics difficult, most candidates gravitated naturally towards the *chinsa* examination which, *inter alia* required the composition of poems.

In spite of the potentially stultifying influence of the imitation of Chinese models, Nansŏrhŏn's lifetime spanned a period of transition in literary tradition, which moved from the influence of Sung (960-1279) to that of T'ang (618-907).[1] The transition seemed inevitable as disillusionment with Confucian literary values emerged and the ideals of the scholar-officials came under scrutiny. The underlying cause of the transition was the influence of the *Fu ku* (Kor. *Pokko*, neo-classical movement), a form of orthodox archaism. The movement advocated that prose must be modeled on the prose of the Ch'in (221-207) or Han (202 B.C.E.-220 C.E.), and that poetry must be modeled on that of the High T'ang (Sheng-T'ang, 734-765). The latter meant that it behooved the poets of the day to strive to emulate the poetry of the High T'ang masters, such as Tu Fu (712-770), Li Po (701-762) and Wang Wei (699-759). A group called *Sam-Tang shiin* (Three T'ang Talents of Korea) fully exploited this new tradition as a means of overcoming the embodiment of neo-Confucian orthodoxy in literature, a requirement which could only be fulfilled at the expense of the spontaneous beauty of literary expression. The group rejected the longstanding attitude that poetry should remain as a pastime for the cultured man, maintaining instead that the study and writing of poetry should exist as a lifelong discipline for writers and that literature must be their major concern. The Hŏ family tutor, Yi Tal (1561-1618, styled Son'gok), was one of this group and it was he and Nansŏrhŏn's brother, Hŏ Pong (1551-1588, styled Hagok), who had the greatest influence on her literary work.

Some two-thirds of Nansŏrhŏn's poems represent the reworking of traditional themes drawn from early Chinese folk-songs. Notwithstanding this however, she developed an indigenous, aesthetic predilection—simple and open-hearted—with lively diction, reinforced by a very vivid imagination. The influence of "Taoism, with its belief in *Hsien* (Kor. *Sŏn*), or transcendent immortals" pervades her works. She was beset by an enduring fantasy of being able to divest herself of worldly shackles and fly beyond the

---

1. *CBYS*, Chapter 9, *Munjang-bu* 文章部 2, Shi 詩 p. 157. See also *HKCS*, p. 467.

stifling universe, where everything seemed to be wrong for her, to the world of the immortals. A further characteristic of her work is her extraordinary melancholy, even when measured by the Chinese or Korean yardstick. Many of her melancholic poems are imbued with the theme of the renounced or neglected lady-figure. The themes are elaborated for the most part through the persona of the *yüeh-fu* (Kor. *akpu)* tradition; some poems express the disenchanted love of a woman for her husband, which can possibly be seen as a reflection of her own feelings.

The Confucian code imposed severe restraints on both the social and intellectual activities of women. Any seemingly untoward conduct was considered to be "evil virtue." Nansŏrhŏn can be grouped with those writers whose literature is known, because of their deprived standing in society as well as their disenchantment with Confucian ethics, as the Literature of the outsiders. Their literature was influenced more by Taoism, with its belief in *hsien* than by either Confucianism or Buddhism or indeed any other philosophy. Nansŏrhŏn's poems are pervaded with the influence of the belief in *hsien* and the *Ch'u tz'u* (The Songs of the South) tradition, and are predominantly melancholic. Nansŏrhŏn's work has occasioned considerable controversy. Some critics accuse her of plagiarism and there is certainly some evidence to support such a charge. The amount however is considered minimal in relation to the total volume of her collection. Other scholars have reasoned that her brother, Hŏ Kyun (1569-1618, styled Kyosan, also known as *Sŏngso),* introduced additional lines when he compiled her collection and made it public, following her death. This too, must remain as conjecture. It seems likely that her *akpu* style poems are the major cause of the controversy. *Akpu,* particularly the new *akpu,* are a recreation of old folk-songs which on occasion adopt the song title itself, thus creating the impression of poetry copied from old established songs. Much of Nansŏrhŏn's poetry was lost, when it was burnt following her death. A sufficient amount has been handed-down however to show that her work has both enriched and modified Sino-Korean poetic language, marking her as a great poet. Her writing on the Taoist immortals has been accepted as the classic of *hsien* Taoist poems in Korea.

Her work, entitled *Nansŏrhŏn chip* (Collected Works of Hŏ Nansŏrhŏn),[2] contains two hundred and fourteen[3] *hanshi* and two pieces of prose. Fifty three of Nansŏrhŏn's poems and one of her prose pieces have been translated and interpreted and these are presented herein, following the order of their appearance in her collected works. Poems have been chosen to represent each thematic or stylistic group. Another, admittedly somewhat subjective, criterion for selection has been how well the poems go over in English.

---

2. See p. 30, below.
3. See p. 32, below.

Finally, I have tried to include pieces that shed light on her personal life. Since only minor research has been undertaken on the analysis of some common phenomena of Chinese poetic structure in her poems, attention is given to both the formal and the non-formal structure, taking into consideration sound, syntax and meaning. As the four tonal changes are not acknowledged in Korean *hanmun*, each character has been checked against a tonal table to identify the tone of each rhyme, as well as the tonal pattern of each verse.

I
Life of Hŏ Nansŏrhŏn

Hŏ Ch'ŏhŭi 許楚姬 [1] (styled Nansŏrhŏn 蘭雪軒) was born in 1563 during the reign of King Myŏngjong (r.1545-1567) of the Chosŏn dynasty. Her birth place was Kangnŭng Special City,[2] located in the picturesque eastern province of Kangwŏn, a region renowned for its mountains and spectacular waterfalls. Some information exists about her family[3] as well as material written by her family in which she is mentioned. Although her whole life revolved around the family domain however, very little has been written about her. The years between her marriage at the age of fifteen and her death are almost wholly unrecorded. Fortunately, what has been passed down does give an insight into Nansŏrhŏn's personality. The considerable difficulty in reconstructing Nansŏrhŏn's biography is largely brought about because the material in her collected works, which could have provided a wealth of information about her life, is largely poems—some 214 in all. Like others of

---

1. It was not common practice for Chosŏn dynasty women to have a given name, except for women with special occupations such as *kisaeng*. This name, Hŏ Ch'ohŭi first appeared in *Haksan ch'odam* 鶴山樵談 by Hŏ Kyun 許筠, and was later cited in such Chinese anthologies as *Ming shih tsung* 明詩宗 and *Lieh ch'ao shih chi* 列朝詩集 as well as in Korean sources. Her courtesy name was Kyŏngbŏn 景樊 (the latter believed to have been taken out of respect for the female Taoist, Lady Fan 樊夫人, of China). Lady Fan appears in *Shen hsien chuan* 神仙傳 as the wife of Liu Kang 劉綱 of the Chin dynasty, who is known as the author of *Hsu hsien chuan* 續仙傳. Legend has it that both husband and wife became immortals. Ko Hung 葛洪 (283-343), *Shen hsien chuan*, Chapter 7, on Lady Fan. *Han Wei ts'ung shu*, 1895 ed.
2. Present Myŏngju County 溟州郡, Kangwŏn Province 江原道.
3. *Myŏngjong Taewang shillok* 明宗大王實錄, *Sŏnjo Sogyŏng Taewang shillok*, 宣祖昭敬大王實錄 *CWS*, vol. 19-25. Chōsen Sōtokufu, *Chōsen tosho kaidai* 朝鮮圖書解題, *Shūbu* 集部, on Hŏ Pong, Hŏ ssi, and Hŏ Kyun, photo-reprint, (Tokyo:1965). Yun Kukhyŏng 尹國馨 (1543-1611), "Munsŏ mannok" 聞韶漫錄 in *TDYS*, *kwŏn* 55, vol. 10, pp. 575-621. Chōsen Sōtokufu, *Chōsen kinseki sōran* 朝鮮金石總攬, Pt. 229, on *Hŏ Yŏp shindobi* 許曄神道碑 (果川), photo-reprint, (Tokyo:1971), 2 vols., vol. 2, pp. 790-95.

her time, she wrote occasional poems marking momentous events such as parting from a brother or her husband and, in a time of deepest grief, the death of her children. Regretfully, these are the only works of Nansŏrhŏn which provide valid biographical information. It is this lack of sound biographical data that has embellished the mystery surrounding her life.

There is nothing to indicate that Nansŏrhŏn's childhood was anything but happy and peaceful. She was drawn closely to her brothers, the elder Hŏ Pong, the younger Hŏ Kyun, and, presumably, also to her half-brother Hŏ Sŏng (1548-1612, styled Angnok) by her father's first marriage. She grew up in a household whose family members were amongst the most illustrious scholars and politicians in the country. The official biographies of Nansŏrhŏn's father and brothers are contained in *Chosŏn Wangjo Shillok* (The Veritable Record of the Chosŏn Dynasty),[4] as well as in other traditional sources. The most comprehensive and reliable biography of Nansŏrhŏn's family is considered to be the epitaph of her father, Hŏ Yŏp (1517-1580), which is located in Ch'odang Village, Shindong Township, Shihŭng County, Kyŏnggi Province.[5] According to the epitaph:

> Hŏ Yŏp styled Ch'odang was born in Yongin County. He was a scholar official who held several distinguished government positions such as Principal of the National Academy (*Sŏnggyun'gwan taesasŏng*),[6] Censor-General, Office of the Censor-General (*Saganwŏn taesagan*),[7] Royal Secretary (*sŭngji*),[8] etc.

Hŏ Yŏp was a distinguished Confucian scholar and writer whose personality and code of honour are reputed to have secured him many admirers. His marriage to a daughter of Prince Sŏp'yŏng (1478-1537) gave him two daughters and a son, Hŏ Sŏng. After his wife's death, Hŏ Yŏp married again, this time, a daughter of the Second Minister of the Board of Rites, a Miss Kim, by whom he had three children, Hagok (Hŏ Pong), Nansŏrhŏn and Kyosan (Hŏ Kyun).[9] The direct line of Nansŏrhŏn can be traced back to the thirteenth century, to Hŏ Kong (Mun'gyŏng kong), who was a distinguished statesman and scholar. Through the generations, the Hŏ of Yangch'ŏn maintained a renowned lineage.[10]

Nansŏrhŏn's half brother, Hŏ Sŏng was also a highly respected scholar and senior government official, holding positions such as Censor-General and Minister of Three Boards—The Board of Rites (*Yejo*), The Board of War (*Pyŏngjo*) and The Board of Personnel (*Ijo*). In 1590 he accompanied the

4. See CWS, vol. 20, p. 19, p. 134, p. 533; vol. 21, p. 159, p. 316, p. 344; vol. 25, p. 487.
5. *Chōsen kinseki sōran*, pp. 790-95.
6. *Ibid.*, p. 132, 571, 615, and *kwŏn* 34. *CWS*, vol. 21, p. 159.
7. See *Myŏngjong shillok*, *kwŏn* 30. *CWS*, vol. 20, p. 533.
8. See *Sŏnjo shillok*, *kwŏn* 7. *CWS*, vol. 21, p. 312.
9. *Sŏnjo shillok*, *kwŏn* 13. *CWS*, vol. 25, p. 487.
10. *KRS*, *kwŏn* 105, *Yŏlchŏn*, *kwŏn* 18 in vol. 3, pp. 313-14. See also *HNCJ*, pp. 521-24.

Royal Envoy to Japan, in the position of Correspondence Officer. On his return, he accurately predicted the invasion of Korea by a Japanese force under Toyotomi Hideyoshi.[11]

Hagok, Nansŏrhŏn's elder brother, was a politician as well as a remarkable writer.[12] However, while holding government office he found himself constantly critical of the government's handling of state affairs, which naturally led to trouble.[13] It was, in fact, his integrity and uncompromising nature that were eventually responsible for his political downfall. For his disobedience he was exiled for three years to the notoriously harsh region of Kapsan.[14] This period of banishment was not entirely wasted, however, as while he was there, he was able to read the works of the High T'ang (*Sheng T'ang*)[15] poets, particularly the work of Li Po. Hagok's own style was simple yet original, disdaining the exigencies of prosody. He later acquired the pseudonym of "Banished Immortal"[16] and came to be accepted as an illustrious writer.[17] He was indeed a prolific writer with his corpus of material including works such as *Hagok choch'ŏn'gi*, *Haedong yasŭng*, and others.

Hagok died at the age of thirty-eight, when Nansŏrhŏn was twenty–six years old and her own demise was only a short time away. Hagok loved his sister dearly and saw great talent and vivacity in her. The two being in harmony, he was in many respects her best tutor. Nansŏrhŏn's love and regard are commemorated in seven poems dedicated to her brother in which she expresses her sorrow for him and resentment of the circumstances which led to his untimely death. The compilation and preservation of Nansŏrhŏn's works however is attributed to her younger brother, Kyosan, who is said to have possessed an extraordinary memory, to the extent of being able to learn and recall several hundred characters in a single day's study. Kyosan came to realize however that true learning lay not in cramming for the government service examination, but rather in following his brother's advice and reading the ancient writings (*komun*).[18] He affirms his thoughts in this regard in a letter to his tutor, the foremost poet of the T'ang style Yi Tal (1561-1618, styled Son'gok).[19]

---

11. *Imjin waeran* 壬辰倭亂 (Japanese Invasion of Korea, 1592-98).
12. *CTGB*, p. 132, 195.
13. He led the *Tongin* 東人 (Easterners) Faction together with Kim Hyowŏn 金孝元 in their feud against the Sŏin 西人 (Westerners) whose leader was Shim Ŭigyŏm 沈義謙 (1535-1587). See also *Chōsen Tosho kaidai*, p. 451.
14. *Chōsen Tosho Kaidai*, p. 451.
15. Hŏ Kyun, *Haksan ch'odam*, *HKCS*, p. 468.
16. Li Po himself was also known as the "Banished Immortal" (*che hsien* 謫仙).
17. For a comprehensive biography of Hagok, see Yun Kukhyŏng's *Munsŏ mannok*. *TDYS*, vol. 10, pp. 612-13.
18. *Komun* 古文 refers to the prose of Ch'in 秦 (221-207 B.C.) and Han 漢 (202 B.C.- 220 A.D.), and poetry of High T'ang 盛唐 (*Sheng-T'ang*).
19. Hŏ Kyun, *Sŏngso pokpugo*, *kwŏn* 10, *Munbu* 文部, 7." Tap Yi saeng sŏ." *HKCS*, p. 122.

The golden opportunity to learn with her brothers was one which Nansŏrhŏn did not let slip by. She studied the Chinese classics known as the *Shu ching* (Book of Documents) and *Shih ching* (Book of Songs), as well as miscellaneous other Chinese works. Her poems clearly illustrate her knowledge of *Pullyu Tugongbushi ŏnhae,* commonly known as *Tushi ŏnhae* (The Korean Annotated Translation of the Complete Works of Tu Fu). It is said there was not a single book in the Ch'odang family library that she had not read,[20] signifying she was her brothers' equal in scholarly pursuits. Nansŏrhŏn's unrestricted reading during her early years, drawing upon the ten thousand or so books in the library,[21] undoubtedly crystallized her thoughts and suggested themes for some of her poetry. Legend has it that she showed such a precocious gift for literature that she produced *Kwanghanjŏn Paegongnu sangnangmun* (Inscriptions on the Ridge Pole of the White Jade Pavilion in the Kwanghan Palace), when only eight years old. This work alone earned her the title of "immortal maiden." Hagok was fully aware of his sister's talent and arranged for Son'gok to teach her T'ang poetry,[22] an opportunity that both guided her to a new literary genre and contributed to her development as an outstanding poet. Kyosan too, held this tutor in high regard and wrote his biography, *Son'gok san'injŏn* (The Biography of Son'gok, the Recluse). It was as a direct result of Son'gok's influence that both Nansŏrhŏn and Kyosan wrote outstanding poetry in the style of the T'ang.[23]

The following extract from the *Biography of Son'gok, the Recluse* also reveals the degree of influence that Son'gok could have exercised on Nansŏrhŏn's writing:

> Yi Tal (Son'gok) was born of a *yangban* father by a *kisaeng* (female entertainer) and was thus destined to have an unfortunate life. Although he was well endowed with talent and a good education, he was barred from serving the State in any high official capacity because of his illegitimate status. He had once held a minor government position but resigned from it and retired to his farmstead, Son'gok. In retirement he studied Li Po and other High T'ang poets. His appearance was always shabby and his wayward spirit refused to let him bow to conventional etiquette. It seems that throughout his life he never set up a home of his own. Instead, wandering from place to place begging his food. The fact that many people despised him neither bothered him nor prevented him from writing his poetry. He felt that he was trapped in an unjust and rigid social system and decided to fight against the injustice and cruelty by writing unconventionally. His many splendid poems are acknowledged as being amongst the most brilliant collections of all the T'ang style poetry written in Korea since the Shilla dynasty.[24]

---

20. The multitude of sources from which she drew her poetic themes prove this to be true.
21. Ch'odang 草堂 is her father's pen name, and thus this Ch'odang Library might be referring to her father's collection.
22. See n.15, p. 7 above.
23. *Ibid.*
24. Hŏ Kyun, *Sŏngso pokpugo,* kwŏn 8, *Mumbu* 5, Biographies. *HKCS* p. 104.

Kyosan (Hŏ Kyun) and Nansŏrhŏn, too, had a common bond in their developing critical views of the social injustices of the period. Similarly, Kyosan and Son'gok seem to have had much in common, for they were both accomplished writers, free-thinkers and impulsive souls by nature. Kyosan himself possessed great feeling and compassion for the deprived classes, including a particularly sympathetic attitude towards the status of women in society. This philanthropic attitude was considered most unusual for a person of Kyosan's background. He held a succession of demanding posts in government, including Minister of the Board of Punishment(*hyŏngjo p'an sŏ*),[25] and Sixth and Seventh State Councillor of the State Council (*ŭijŏngbu chwau ch'amch'an*).[26] Included amongst his works are the famous *Hong Kiltong chŏn* (The Tale of Hong Kiltong),[27] as well as *Chang san'injŏn*,[28] *Namgung sŏnsaeng chŏn*[29] and *Changsaeng chŏn*.[30] He excelled however in the writing of poetry and in literary criticism. His *Sŏngsu shihwa*[31] and *Haksan ch'odam* are the two most valuable and crucial sources for the study of Chosŏn dynasty poetry. He was also the compiler of *Kukcho shisan*,[32] a collection of poems written by thirty-five poets of the early to mid-Chosŏn dynasty, with its excellent commentary on poets and poetic tradition. Kyosan was also a political reformist and advocated revolution within the socially-deprived class of *Sŏŏl* (the illegitimates). These activities involved him in political feuds for which he was banished many times. Finally, in 1618 (some twenty-eight years after Nansŏrhŏn's death) he was executed for treason.[33] By every account, Kyosan was a remarkable man—proud, principled, highly emotional and impulsive as well as being an earnest believer in social justice.

The leading critic of the late Chosŏn dynasty, Hwang Hyŏn (1855-1910, styled Maech'ŏn), in his poetic discourse *Tokkukcho chegashi* (On Reading Poems by Various Poets of Chosŏn Dynasty) affirmed "the three jewels" of the Hŏ family to be the foremost group of writers during the Chosŏn dynasty, referring particularly to Nansŏrhŏn, whom he considered the most outstanding of the three.[34] Hagok, Nansŏrhŏn and Kyosan are also included in the literature section of the *Chŏn'go taebang*, *kwŏn* 3, Munjangga, (The Directory of Great Philosophers).

---

25. *Kwanghaejo ilgi*, *kwŏn* 3. *TDYS*, vol. 8, p. 347.
26. *Ibid*, p. 442, 531
27. See Hŏ Kyun, *Hong Kiltong chŏn* 洪吉童傳. *HKCS*, pp. 3-40 (2nd group).
28. These epic style essays are contained in Hŏ Kyun's *Sŏngso pokpugo*, *kwŏn* 8, Munbu, 5. *HKCS*, pp. 104-11.
29. *Ibid*., pp. 105-110.
30. *Ibid*., pp. 110-111.
31. See Hŏ Kyun, *Sŏngso pokpugo*, *kwŏn* 25, *Sŏlbu* 說部 4, "Sŏngsu shihwa." *HKCS*, pp. 234-43.
32. Hŏ Kyun, *Kukcho shisan*, pp. 239-651.
33. Hŏ Kyun and Yi Ich'ŏm 李爾瞻 (1560-1623) jointly suggested the removal from office of Queen Mother Inmok 仁穆大妃, the second wife of King Sŏnjo, but later Hŏ Kyun was betrayed by Yi Ich'ŏm. See *Kwanghaejo ilgi* 光海朝日記, *kwŏn* 4. *TDYS*, pp. 542-46.
34. *NSC*, p. 326.

Nansŏrhŏn had early visions of becoming a great scholar, but soon realized that it was not to be. She is believed to have been married at about fifteen years of age[35] to the son of a civil official, Kim Sŏngnip (1562-1592)[36] of the Andong Kim lineage, an equally distinguished family. Kim Sŏngnip studied constantly from the time of his marriage and passed the Civil Service Examination in the year of Nansŏrhŏn's death. Nevertheless, he was unable to match his wife either in scholarly achievement or literary talent. It is said that he was an unimposing man, and a philanderer, showing all the frustration of subjugation to his wife's superiority. This repression kept him at a distance and often away from home. Indeed, his studies at the Reading Hall[37] were often mere excuses for absence from home while seeking the favours of another woman. Many of Nansŏrhŏn's poems exemplify her heart-felt sorrow, in their depictions of the loneliness of a neglected wife.

With so much misery in her marriage,[38] it is hardly surprising that melancholy and despair are so deeply reflected in her verse. To compound her misery and frustration, she never found favour with her mother-in-law, as revealed by Kyosan in his *Sŏngso pokpugo*.[39] The combination of physical beauty and superior talent, coupled with a background of high education and an outstanding family, must have posed a real problem for Nansŏrhŏn in her efforts to adapt herself to the ideal image of a woman cast in the Chosŏn society mould. Here was a singular woman who read the classics widely and who was influenced more by Taoism than by either Confucianism or Buddhism.[40] She was, nevertheless, like all her contemporaries, confined to the inner quarters of the house. With these facts in mind, it is not difficult to understand why a substantial proportion of her poetry, more than half, attempts to capture the dream-world and the visionary land of the immortals. The harsh conditions imposed by her confined and anxious existence in the real world apparently make it easier for her thoughts to enter the imaginary world of the immortals, which she seems to do constantly. Unable, of course, to transform her mortal condition to the supernatural, she satisfies her desires by expressing her sentiments in the writing of mystical poems.

---

35. According to *Sŏnjo shillok, kwŏn* 13. *CWS*, vol. 25, p. 487, her father died in 1580, which makes Nansŏrhŏn seventeen. On the same page Kim Sŏngnip is recorded as a son-in-law of Hŏ Yŏp, indicating that Nansŏrhŏn was already married at that time.

36. *Kukcho pangmok* 國朝榜目, photo-reprint ed., (Seoul:Taehan Min'guk Kukhoe Tosŏgwan, 1971), p. 163. See also Mun Kyŏnghyŏn, "Nansŏrhŏn yŏng'u." Kugŏ Kungmunhakhoe, *Hammunhak yŏn'gu* 漢文學 研究, p. 318.

37. In 1426 King Sejong established a system granting young civil officials study leave to pursue further research in their respective fields. To this end, he established a reading hall where they could concentrate on their studies without distraction.

38. Hŏ Kyun, *Haksan Ch'odam. HKCS* p. 470.

39. See Hŏ Kyun, *Sŏngso pokpugo, kwŏn* 3, *pubu* 賦部, 31, sa 辭, *HKCS*, p. 73.

40. See Chapter III, part 2 below.

Several devastating blows hit Nansŏrhŏn in a relatively short space of time. Her two children, a girl and a boy, died in consecutive years. The children's tiny tombs were placed in the family tumulus of the Kim of Andong clan (which has Nansŏrhŏn's tomb immediately to the rear). The location is in the present Kyŏngsu, commonly called Kyŏngshi Village, Ch'owŏl Township, Kwangju County, Kyŏnggi Province.[41] From the time of these tragedies, until her own untimely death, she had to contend with increasing disappointment in her husband; resentment from her mother-in-law; the exile and eventual death of her dearest brother, Hagok and her own indifferent health. A poem reputed to have been written by one of her husband's acquaintances, but circulated as if written by Nansŏrhŏn, reads:

> I wish to bid farewell to Kim Sŏngnip in this mortal world,
> And join Tu Mu forever in the world to come.

This line was intended simply to ridicule Nansŏrhŏn's husband. Some however, took it seriously and concluded that her courtesy name Kyŏngbŏn was taken in deference to her longing for the outstanding Late T'ang poet, Tu Mu (803-853, styled Fan-ch'uan), who had the reputation of being a handsome man.[42] This, however, is completely unfounded, and it is generally accepted that Nansŏrhŏn took the name of Kyŏngbŏn out of respect for the female Taoist, Lady Fan,[43] who together with her husband was supposed to have become an immortal.

After Nansŏrhŏn's death, Kim Sŏngnip remarried but died during the *Imjin Waeran* (The Japanese Invasion of Korea, 1592-1598), while leading the *Chŏngŭigun* (Righteous Army). His body was never found, only his garments, buried in its place. The tomb lies next to that of his second wife, leaving Nansŏrhŏn in a lone grave. Kim Sŏngnip, the eldest son of the Andong Kims, died without an heir, and his younger brother Chŏngnip had his son, Kim Chin (a governor of Kangwŏn Province),[44] adopted posthumously by Kim Sŏngnip in order to continue the lineage. His present-day descendants are said to be still living in Kyŏngshi Village.[45]

Nansŏrhŏn's official biography as recorded in the epilogue of *Collected Works of Nansŏrhŏn* (*Nansŏrhŏn chip*)[46] is written by Hŏ Kyun, and is one of the few reliable sources on her life.

---

41. Nam Pyŏngyun, "Hŏ Nansŏrhŏn ŭi hanshi yŏn'gu" (unpublished M.A. thesis, Kyemyŏng University, Seoul, 1972), p. 38.
42. Pak Chiwŏn (1737-1805, styled Yŏnam) in his *Yŏrha ilgi* 熱河日記 acknowledges the fact that Kim Sŏngnip's friends used to tease him (in the same context as referred above).
43. Kim Manjung, *Sŏp'o manp'il* 西浦漫筆, part 2, *op. cit.*, p. 628.
44. *HNCJ*, pp. 523-524.
45. Nam Pyŏngyun, *op. cit.*, p. 11.
46. See Hŏ Kyun's Pal (Epilogue) in *Nansŏrhŏn chip. CYYMJ*, p. 23.

The author's name was Miss Hŏ, styled Nansŏrhŏn. She was my third elder sister and was married to an Eighth Counsellor of the Office of the Special Counsellors (*Hongmun'gwan chŏjak*), Kim Sŏngnip (1562-1592), but she died very young. Being childless, she could afford to spend much of her time writing, and consequently accumulated a great deal of literary work. However, according to her wishes, her works were burned and only a small portion, my own transcriptions, has survived. I have kept them for a long time, but have now engraved them on wood, as I fear losing them, and because I wish to introduce Nansŏrhŏn's works to a wider circle of readers.

> 1st—10th day of 4th month, 1608
> Hŏ Kyun, the younger brother
> at P'iu-dang Hall

Hŏ Kyun's anguish at the loss of his sister is expressed in his work, *Sŏngso pokpugo:*[47]

Song of Broken Jade

Preface

My late sister was a virtuous lady, possessed with exceptional literary talent. However, she was unable to win over her mother-in-law. Furthermore, she lost both of her children and harboured resentment, eventually bringing about her own death.

Whenever I think of her, I feel an uncontrollable pain. Once I read "Huang T'ai-shih tz'u" in which the author's grief at the loss of his beloved sister, Miss Huang, was most intense. Since the grief of losing our sister was so similar, in spite of the gap of a thousand years, I pour out my sorrow here, imitating his verse, "Song of Broken Jade."

Song

> Your life was imperfect,
> Like broken jade or pearls fallen into pieces.
> Heaven endowed you generously with your talent,
> Why then has it recklessly punished you with such cruelty
> And snatched you away in such a hurry?
> Your harp and lute lie dusty and unplayed;
> Though there are delicacies you cannot taste them.
> Your silent bedchamber looks so bleak;
> The iris sprouts were destroyed by the frost.
> May your soul return to roam here!
> How sad that you were spared for only a fleeting moment
>   in this uncertain world.

---

47. Hŏ Kyun, *Sŏngso pokpugo*, chapter 3, *pu* section 1, part 2, *sa, HKCS*, p. 73.

You came like a flash and left us as suddenly;
Time flows ceaselessly.
The clouds gently drift over the Kwangnŭng tomb path;
A shadow in daylight and the palace of the ghost.
Blown by the wind in the dense forest, the dark unseen world.
Where will the departed spirit eventually go?
The Jasper Isles must be far away. Where is the jade tower?
May you come back to roam
And I shall follow you cheerfully to diverse mountains.
May your spirit wander in this world;
And with myriads of other spirits depart into distant
    clouds.
When you leave make the rainbow your banner,
    the phoenix your carriage.
Hold audience with the Highest in Heaven,
Driven by the chariot of cold and strong wind,
When you pour the wine to Hsi Wang-mu at Emerald Pond
    the three lights shine beneath you.
When you look down on this world
I must control my sorrow.
And when I gaze at Heaven my heart is tormented.
May you come back from time to time
    and saunter in the garden of the Highest.

Again, in his work *Haksan ch'odam* (1593)[48] he reiterates his sorrow:

My sister also used to write poems in her dreams, one of which reads:

The Sapphire Sea flows into the Emerald Lake;
The blue phoenix mingles with multicoloured one(s).
Twenty-seven lotus flowers:
Scarlet petals fall under the frosty moon.

She died the following year. Three nines are twenty-seven and it is the same number of years my sister has enjoyed this life. When human affairs are pre-ordained, how can one avoid one's allotted destiny? My sister's poems are all heaven-sent. She enjoyed writing, "Wandering Immortals." Her poetic diction is always so refreshing to the point that it is something no ordinary mortal could attain. Her writing is marvellous and her twenty-four most beautiful prose pieces bearing the title of "Inscription on the Ridge Pole of White Jade Tower in the Kwanghan Palace" are well known.

48. *HKCS*, pp. 470, 474, 484.

My brother (Pong) once said that Kyŏngbŏn's (Nansŏrhŏn) talent could not be attained through study alone. She inherited much from Li Po or Li Ho of China in her verses. Alas, her life was lacking in conjugal harmony. When alive, parental enjoyment was cut short by her children's early death and when she died, she left no offspring to carry on the ancestral rites. Grief for such a broken jade knows no bounds.

My sister once professed that when she wrote *sa* (Ch. *tz'u*) the lines all followed the same pattern. She enjoyed writing short pieces. I thought it an achievement beyond human endeavour, but when I saw her poems and illustrated music book there was a punctuation mark by the side of each character. She reasoned that certain words had voiceless unaspirated initials (*chŏnch'ŏng*) or voiceless aspirated initials (*panch'ŏng*) while certain characters had voiced obstruents such as stops, affricates, fricatives etc. (*chŏnt'ak*) or voiced sonorants (*pant'ak*). Testing her theory, I took the words and characters she had defined and tried to match them. Although there were a few discrepancies, by and large there were no serious errors. It was then I realized my sister had an unparalleled genius. Since that time I have paid homage (to her talent) and followed her. From her pen, even the barest effort produced a great achievement. In her poem, "Fisherman's Home" all the rhymes are regulated, except for one word which is not a full rhyme. The poem reads:

"Fisherman's Home"

In the courtyard a sad eastern wind blows,
A tree over the fence is white with peach blossoms.
Leaning against the jade rail she yearns for home,
She cannot return.
Luxuriant foliage of fragrant plants merge into the sky.
Silk draperies and beautiful windows are shut and deserted.
Two streams of tears on the powdered face soak the
   scarlet blossom.
Beyond the misty trees north and south of the river.
Love does not end.
The mountains are long, the water is wide;
   news does not come.

(All the rhymes are in deflected tone.)

Hŏ Kyun continues:

Nansŏrhŏn should have used the moderated (half) dull sound in the place of the word *chu* 朱 (scarlet), the sound of which is absolutely dull. She should, of course, be excused the aberration, as even a gifted man like Su Tung-p'o could not regulate the sounds by force and she did not have his talent!

Hŏ Kyun then dealt with another of Nansŏrhŏn's works, "Song of a Walk in Skyland:"

Poem 1

By night she rides a phoenix to the Blessed Isles,
On a chariot drawn by unicorns over jade grass.
A sea breeze blows, scattering the jade peach blossoms;[49]
The jade tray is filled with the dates of An-ch'i.[50]

In Hŏ Kyun's words:

This was an imitation of Liu Yu-hsi's Pu hsu tz'u "Song on Pacing the Void." Also, the one hundred exquisitely pure pieces of "Wandering Immortals" by Nansŏrhŏn, are all in Kuo P'u's style and as such, something Ts'ao T'ang and others would not have been able to match. According to my brother and Yi Ikchi, the idea that all (of her poems) are imitations is hasty and lacking in perception. My sister's supreme talent is well-recognized."

Yu Sŏngnyong's epilogue to Nansŏrhŏn's collection:[51]

My friend Hŏ Misuk (Hŏ Pong) possesseed extraordinary talent, but unfortunately he died young. I read his surviving works and could not resist striking the table in admiration. One day, his younger brother Tanbo (Hŏ Kyun) brought in a manuscript written by their sister, Nansŏrhŏn, and gave it to me to read. I was amazed by it and exclaimed, "It's extraordinary." These are not a woman's works. How is it there are so many unusual talents in the Hŏ family?

I am ignorant about poetry. But if I must criticize what I have seen—her placing of words and creation of ideas are like flowers in the moon reflected in water. They are so bright and elegant that it is more than I can grasp and appreciate. The chiming sounds are like those of jade pieces brushing against each other. The poems are as lofty as Mount Sung and Mountain Hu competing with each other for prominence. They are like autumn lotus pulled out of the water, like spring clouds in a beautiful sky.

Within her galaxy of talent, the highest points are derived from Han and Wei and there is a good measure which competes with the High T'ang. She had a capacity to consider both the abstract and the practical, such as her feelings towards things and thoughts on the one hand, and on the other, her deep concern

---

49. The peaches said to grow in the K'un-lun Mountains and to be served at P'an- t'ao Hui, the periodical banquet of the Immortals.
50. An-ch'i (An-ch'i Sheng) 安期生: a magician from the Shantung coast favoured by the first Ch'in Emperor. He disappeared, leaving a letter in which he invited the emperor to meet him in two years' time in the fairy island of P'eng-lai. The imposter Li Shiao-chün 李小君 boasted to Emperor Wu of the Han dynasty that he had been to sea and saw An-ch'i Sheng eating dates as big as melons. See David Hawkes, "The Quest of the Goddess" in Cyril Birch, *Studies in Chinese Literary Genres* (Berkeley:1974), p. 179, 200.
51. *NSC*, pp. 322-323.

for events of the times and the social conditions. Such attributes are generally in accordance with the style of patriots and heroes and usually far removed from the common people. Even if the "Cypress Boat" (poem in the *Shih ching*) does conquer the Land East of the Sea (Korea), it won't be able to monopolize the beauty on the front page!

I told Tanbo to take them home, to put them in order and to safeguard them as a treasure, to edit them and to add a chronicle as a family instruction, so that they would be handed down through the generations to come."

Sŏae (Yu Sŏngnyong) wrote this at home in Seoul, Mid-winter, 1591.

II
The Sino-Korean Poetic Tradition
of the Late Sixteenth Century

Introduction

During the early period (1392-1567) of the Chosŏn dynasty poetry continued
in the Koryŏ convention, influenced by Sung poetry. However towards the
end of the sixteenth century the *hanshi* poets began to shift their attention to
T'ang poetry. This era is roughly defined as 1568-1674. The early Chosŏn
dynasty, though of vital importance in the growth of social and political
institutions in Korea, shows a mere continuation of the preceding dynasty's
genres and styles in the field of literature. In a broad sense, the characteristic
feature of early Chosŏn dynasty literature was that it was a Confucian
literature developed by the literati officials. These officials were the writers
and arbiters as well as the readers of literature. Through them Confucianism
moulded the Korean literary character of the period.

The literary tradition of the mid-sixteenth century (the reign of King
Chungjong, r. 1506-1544) is divided into three categories — *Sajang* (polished
style) School or *Hun'gu* School (literature of the bureaucrats), the *Sarim* or
Sallim School (literature of rustic literati),[1] and "literature of the outsiders."
The first two follow the Confucian tradition, while the third is anti-
Confucian.[2] *Sallim* scholars were strict followers of Chu Hsi's neo-Confucian

---

1. The *Sarim* 士林派 or *Sallim* 山林派 School refers to a group of neo-Confucian scholars and
writers, drawn from the countryside, particularly the south-eastern provinces of North and South
Kyŏngsang, as indicated by the words *Sarim* (Literati of the Forest) or *Sallim* (Mountain and
Forest). They maintained strong resistance to the *Sajang* 詞章派 School.
2. Cho Tong-il, *Han'guk munhak t'ongsa*, 5 vols, (Seoul: Chishik Sanŏp Sa, 1989), vol. 2, pp.
240-391.

orthodoxy (Kor. *Sŏngni* School). They tended to be young and bright but from "out-of-power" clans, whereas the *Sajang* scholars were conservatives who held positions in government offices just as their forebears had done for generations. This *Sajang* tradition encouraged all aspirants for office to acquire considerable proficiency in the composition of poetry. The fifteenth and sixteenth centuries saw an increase in the popularity of poetry. To become a successful statesman meant that one had to be well versed in classical Chinese, as government documents, particularly diplomatic communicatons with China, were written in Classical Chinese, and these had to meet the Chinese standard.

Confucianism, with its vast influence on the Korean people, influenced literature in at least two ways: it affected the lives and ideas of those writers who followed the Confucian code as well as those who reacted against it. Success in personal life strengthened belief in the Confucian orthodoxy. The disappointment that accompanied failure fostered inner rebellion against Confucian orthodoxy, or prompted writers to look to other religions such as Buddhism or Taoism. These rebels deviated from the Confucian norm and in so doing, created a new literary tradition called the "Literature of the Outsiders."

Confucian literature of the early Chosŏn period: *Sajan* School and *Sallim* School

Both *Sajang* and *Sallim* School writers were faithful followers of the Confucian tradition. For them, literature was a vehicle for conveying Confucian teaching in order to encourage the public to emulate Confucian virtues. Such writers emphasised the importance of the study of the Confucian classics and warned against distractions such as the influence of Lao tzu or Chuang tzu. This literature, based on Confucian ethics, formed the mainstream of literary convention. Literati officials were the bureaucrats in the central government and at the same time, the landlords of private estates in the countryside. While in government office they served the country and wrote literature worthy of great statesmen, but when out of office—retired or dismissed—they retreated to their estates and indulged in pastoral literature.[3] At the inception of the Chosŏn dynasty, the literati officials were divided in their loyalties. One group supported the new dynasty and assisted in its establishment, while the other group stayed faithful to the previous dynasty, members of the group passively resisting the transition, often retreating into retirement as a sign of their disapproval. It was this rift that led to the formation of the two separate literary schools.

---

3. Yi Usŏng 李佑成, "Koryŏ mal Yijo ch'o ŭi ŏbuga 高麗末 李朝의 漁父歌, " *Sŏnggyun'gwan Taehakkyo nonmunjip*, vol. 9, p. 125.

The *Sajang* scholars saw their literary art as being of equal importance to the study of neo-Confucian orthodoxy, not only because of their duty to write dignified and well-polished diplomatic documents for their government's relations with China, but also because of their desire to assist in promoting the image of the new dynasty. Although the *Sajang* scholars played a vital role in the development of social and political institutions, both through their publications and the invention of *han'gŭl*, their literature was excessively stylised, crippling creativity of both thought and image. If anything, it became increasingly mannered and rigid in style as the dynasty moved out of its embryonic state. Its members maintained the strong conviction that a poet should not try to create, but should content himself with the study of the ancient writings, and by emulating the best qualities of those writings, bring his own work to perfection.

Sallim School adherents deplored the literary convention of the bureaucrats, criticising the excessive stylisation of their poetry as well as its dullness in choice of both subject and content. Above all, *Sallim* scholars put great emphasis on the function of literature in the context of the neo-Confucian state and society. It was natural for them to oppose the *Sajang* scholars who held all the worthwhile government posts. In order to justify their eremetic lifestyle, the *Sallim* scholars argued the importance of studying neo-Confucian metaphysics in isolation, away from fame and fortune. They considered the literary art as a branch of their scholarship. *Sallim* poetry reflected the tensions inherent in the pursuit of the eremetic life as well as the ambiguities that often surrounded the motives of the men who adopted it. Most of these scholar officials later returned to a public position or at least anxiously awaited the call to do so. Thus, the sincerity of many of the *Sallim* School was open to question. *Sallim* poets regarded the function of literature as being wholly to serve some didactic and political purpose in the context of neo-Confucian orthodoxy. Accordingly, their poetry gave a clear reflection of their philosophical observations.

After two violent purges of the literati, *Muo Sahwa* and *Kapcha Sahwa* (Calamities of scholars in 1494 and 1504), carried out by his predecessor, Prince Yŏnsan (r. 1494-1506), King Chungjong attempted to ensure the revival of the study of neo-Confucian classics. He believed neglect of Confucian studies was the major cause of decline in morality in society. The literary arts of this period emerged only as an adjunct to classical learning, clearly not fertile ground for great and imaginative literature. Disillusionment with Confucian literary values and the ideals of the literati officials began to appear in the mid-sixteenth century.

Move Towards Transition and the Three T'ang Talents of Korea

The publication of two major works in the late fifteenth century, *Tŏngmunsŏn*, 1478 (Anthology of Korean Literature) and *Tushi ŏnhae*, 1491 (Korean Annotated Translation of the Complete Works of Tu Fu) was a crucial influence in the shift of literary conventions away from the long standing Sung tradition, although the actual shift occurred much later. It was not until the late sixteenth century that the tradition of some two hundred years of Sung poetic influence,[4] particularly that of Su Shih (1036-1101, styled Tung-p'o) and Huang T'ing-chien (1045-1105) was replaced by the earlier models of the T'ang period. This shift was due not only to the influence of the two publications mentioned above, but also to the *Sallim* scholars' power-gain in the government which made the transition possible. The *Sallim* scholars who managed to secure positions in government service during the late sixteenth century (King Sŏnjo's reign) were now in a position to compromise the differences existing in the two Confucian literary schools. This was long overdue. The Councillor of the State Council and prominent poet, Pak Sun (1523-89), who was originally a member of the *Sallim* School, proposed that this could be achieved if writers would adopt the poetic traditions of the T'ang in preference to those of the Sung. This proposition was fully accepted by the "Three T'ang Talents of Korea": the poets Ch'oe Kyŏngch'an (1539-83), Paek Kwanghun (1537-82) and Yi Tal (1561-1618, styled Son'gok). Pak Sun called for the abolition of excessive stylisation and content ambiguity, with poets restoring the convention of the natural expression of human feelings. This had a pronounced effect as well as lasting influence on Ch'oe, Pak and Yi. Subsequent development of the new model however moved towards sterile didacticism.

The two prominent literary critics of the sixteenth century, Yi Sugwang (1563-1628, styled Chibong) and Hŏ Kyun refer to this change of direction in Korean poetry. Yi Sugwang in his *Chibong yusŏl*, 1614 and Hŏ Kyun in his *Kukcho shisan*, 1697 (posthumously published) record how Korean poets had revered Su Shih and Huang T'ing-chien since the dynasty began and depended greatly on imitating the features of their poetry as essential qualities to be embodied in their own work. This eventually became slavish imitation, embracing even the foremost Confucian writers who fell into the trap at the expense of original thought and composition. The emergence of Ch'oe Kyŏngch'an and Paek Kwanghun following their study of T'ang poetry resulted in a long overdue change of poetic direction. Their work was emulated by their contemporaries, and the impetus resulted in a change of tradition.[5]

---

4. *HKCS*, p. 467.
5. Yi Sugwang, *CBYS*, chapter 9, *Munjang-bu*, p. 157. See also Hŏ Kyun, *op. cit.*, p. 467.

Hŏ Kyun explains:

Whereas in ancient times literature was the medium for moral instruction and was carefully written to benefit both the populace and the government, and the tendency was to divide literature between literary composition and moral content, this has been detrimental in that diction (or the art of literary skill) has assumed greater importance than the actual content of the literature, thereby effectively damaging true literature.[6]

Two points emerge from this assertion. Firstly, Hŏ Kyun held the firm opinion that regardless of the writer's philosophy, literature should serve as a vehicle for his moral message. Unbiased himself towards any single philosophy, his own writings reveal that he accepted a combination of Buddhism, Taoism and Confucianism, as indeed did many of his contemporaries.[7] Secondly, the art of literary composition was for him an integral part of literature. He also argued however, that as long as the writer had superior moral principles to instil, suitable composition would flow spontaneously. For him and Yi Sugwang, a poem was more than simply an expression of feeling. It was also an expression of sound intellect—a reaction to the conditions of society and their moral nature, recognising the importance of the art of literary expression. The writing of verse was not simply a hobby for the literati officials. It was rather a lifelong discipline of writers for whom literature was the main occupation.

Many poems of the T'ang are in *yüeh-fu* style. During the early T'ang, these *yüeh-fu* poems covered a narrow range of conventional themes including the neglected woman, the frontier soldier, peasant girls, and the bravo (*yu-hsieh*). The majority of *yüeh-fu* had their origins in earlier folk-songs. Up to the middle of the eighth century, many poets continued to write *yüeh-fu* in the early T'ang style, which was then transformed into an essentially High T'ang poetic repertoire. This then developed in two directions. One was *yüeh-fu* written to the music brought back from Central Asia with a new title, and the other was the assimilation of popular songs to *yüeh-fu* under old tune titles. Most of the latter *yüeh-fu* were written predominantly in five-syllable and seven-syllable forms, and thus are indistinguishable from the ordinary *shih* (Kor. *shi*), at least in line form. As a result of this reworking of themes from earlier and current folk-songs, early

---

6. *HKCS*, p. 132.
7. In Korea, the entwinement of Buddhism, Confucianism and Taoism can be traced back to the Shilla period. Ch'oe Ch'iwŏn 崔致遠 (857-?) describes how these three separate religious precepts influenced the Korean *hwarang-do* 花郎道, in his contribution to the preface of Nangnang's 鸞郎 epitaph. This blending was an ever-changing but persistent phenomenon which, during the Chosŏn dynasty, found its way into literary works. See Kim Pushik 金富軾, *Samguk sagi* 三國史記, (Yi Pyŏngdo [ed. and tr.], 2 vol., [Seoul, 19771), *kwŏn* 4, *Shilla pon'gi* 4, on King Chinhŭng (r. 540-76).

T'ang poems on the whole showed much less creativity in theme, although their formal innovations and refinements are important.

The T'ang poets developed and refined a new poetic form called *chin-t'i shih* (Kor. *kŭnch'e shi,* modern-style verse). In this new form, the poets paid careful attention to tonal pattern based on the euphonic principles called *pa ping* (eight faults). These were designed to guard the poets against eight undesirable effects in writing poetry. Of the modern-style verse, *lü shih* (Kor. *yulshi,* regulated verse), and *chüeh-chu* (Kor. *chŏlgu,* quatrains) are the most important. Regulated verse observes, for example, rules controlling line and syllabic content, tonal pattern and strict verbal parallelism. A quatrain obeys less rigid rules. It should consist of four lines and observe only certain rules of regulated verse, i.e. tonal parallelism, but not strict verbal parallelism. After the development of the modern-style, the earlier form was referred to as *ku-shih* (Kor. *koshi,* old-style verse). Unbound by such restrictions as a set number of lines, or tonal and verbal parallelism, this latter form was still used to write *yüeh-fu* poems. Indeed old-style verse was brought to maturity by the T'ang poets.

The "Three T'ang Talents of Korea" sought to interest a much wider range of society in their work. Their poetry turned away from the customary social and philosophical discourse and towards a skilful expression of the poets' intense personal feelings, enveloping such diverse themes as romantic and unrequited love, the eremetic life style, nature's scenic beauty, Taoism and fantasy. Their simple and uncluttered poetic language challenged stylisation and ambiguity. Although this convention had been attempted earlier by the *Sallim* scholar-poet, Pak Sun, it was the "Three T'ang Talents" who brought it to maturity.

The scholars of the Chosŏn dynasty seem to have been at variance in their remarks in regard to the standard which was achieved by the poets of the late sixteenth century in the T'ang poetic tradition. For example, Yi Sugwang did not give them much credit when he said:

> The standard the "Three T'ang Talents" have really achieved is nothing more than an imitation of late T'ang poems and much inferior to the High T'ang. It seems they lack the capability for writing such fine poems as the High T'ang.

This comment meets with the approval of most scholars.[8]

Hŏ Kyun, however, rated the "Three T'ang Talents" very highly, especially Yi Tal.[9]

---

8. *CBYS*, p. 157.
9. *HKCS*, p. 104.

"Literature of the Outsiders": Away from Confucian Literature

Long before the appearance of those literary critics who championed the independence of literature from the classics and who pointed to the inappropriateness of literature as a guide to conduct, there existed a group of poets whose works had moved away from traditional Confucian values. The members of this group, known as the "outsiders," were writers who gave every indication of being able to produce fine work, fitting them well for careers as scholars and officials. They were nevertheless denied the opportunity to participate officially in the important affairs of the period. Unlike the *Sallim* scholars, who had their country estates to rely on when they were out of government office, most of the "outsiders" were from a socially-deprived class, for the most part *sŏŏl* (the illegitimate). Although they had both the talent and the opportunity to learn, they were barred from participation in government affairs because of their inferior social standing. It was natural therefore that their hostility towards the established bureaucracy and the neo-Confucian ideology which supported the system, should run very deep. Their writings openly challenged Confucian ethics; unfortunately however, they did not carry any influence, either socially or politically.

The Chosŏn dynasty regime suppressed any religion or ideology which was thought to stand in the way of the neo-Confucianisation of the state. The "outsiders" rebelled by turning to *Hsien* Taoism as they moved away from established decorum. The "outsiders" and the "Three T'ang Talents" had a common ideal in advocating that poetry should serve as an unrestrained expression of human feeling. A significant difference, however, was that the "outsiders" used the medium of poetry to manifest social protest and not as literature for its own sake. In other words, in contrast to the "Three T'ang Talents," their writing was not so much a vocation. The "outsiders" wrote on such common themes as the injustices of society and the plight of the *ch'ŏnmin*, and other deprived groups. Also reflected in their work was a strong vein of personal dissatisfaction and disillusionment with life. Kim Shisŭp (1435-93, styled Maewŏl-tang), who was the perfect model of a free and individual poet, Ŏ Mujŏk, (fl. 1501, styled Nangsŏn) and Chŏng Hŭiryang (1469-?) are considered as the founders of "literature of the outsiders." Kim Shisŭp was a renowned philosopher as well as a writer. He was also well-known as a Buddhist and as a Taoist, and the intermix of his beliefs and experiences is well preserved in his writings. Principally, he was an outstanding writer, whose works are more influenced by *Hsien* Taoism than any other philosophy or religion. Kim Shisŭp is named by Hong Manjong (1643-1725) in his work called *Sunoji*,[10] as one of the four

---

10. Hong Manjong洪萬宗, *Sunoji* 旬五志. *Hong Manjong chŏnjip* 洪萬宗全集, (photo-reprint ed., 2 vols, Seoul: T'aehaksa, 1980), vol. 1, pp. 1-122.

outstanding scholars of *Hsien* Taoism. Legend has it that Kim eventually found immortality after learning and teaching alchemy and Taoist yoga. His works include *Kŭmo shinhwa*; (New tales from Mt. Kŭmo) and *Maewŏltang chip* (Collections of writings of Maewŏl-tang).[11]

Ŏ Mujŏk was a former slave who had been set free. He was skilled in writing poetry and his poems are included in anthologies such as *Kukcho shisan*. This work records that Ŏ Mujŏk wrote a poem in which he condemned the corruption of the magistrate of his county. Legend says he fled to another county to avoid arrest for his libellous poem and later died there.[12] Chŏng Hŭiryang was a bureaucrat who had been dismissed from his position. Unlike most literati officials who were in the same unfortunate situation, he could not settle in pastoral isolation or adapt his writings to relate to the countryside. His resentful and wandering spirit drove him to extreme pessimism, which manifested itself in his poems as outbursts of his dissatisfaction and disillusionment with life.[13]

It is pertinent to refer again to the poetess Nansŏrhŏn, who as we have already seen, was tormented by the conflict between her role as a woman of a *yangban* family in a rigid Confucian society and her passion to break down social barriers. Frustrated, she turned to the world of the immortals for consolation. Her work is pervaded with the influence of *Hsien* Taoism and in this sense her poetry belongs to the literature of the "outsiders." However, unlike the majority of this group, whose purpose in writing poetry was to protest bitterly against social injustice, Nansŏrhŏn developed an aesthetic approach and wrote poetry for its own sake. Her poetry was influenced more by the literary tradition of the "Three T'ang Talents" than by strictly Confucian literature, and her melancholic love poems remind us that she also emulated the Six Dynasties love poems.

Influence of *Hsien* Taoism on the "Literature of the Outsiders"

The important influence on the "Literature of the outsiders" is *Hsien* Taoism, with its indigenous shamanistic roots. During the reigns of King Chungjong and King Sŏnjo, *Tanhak* (Taoist Alchemy) and *Sŏnp'ung* (the Immortality Cult) became widespread.[14] The Taoist religion had never developed seriously enough to call for the setting up of temples, nor did it produce its

---

11. Kim Shisŭp 金時習, *Maewŏl-tang chip* 梅月堂集 (Sejong Taewang Kinyŏm Saŏphoe, *Kugyŏk Maewŏl-tang chip*, 3 vols., Seoul: 1982)
_____, *Kŭmo shinhwa* 金鰲新話.
12. See Hŏ Kyun, *Kukcho shisan* 國朝詩刪, pp. 288-89, 390. See also Richard Rutt, "Traditional Korean Poetry Criticism," *Transactions* of the Korea Branch of the Royal Asiatic Society, vol. 47 (1974), pp. 126-7.
13. See Hŏ Kyun, *Kukcho shisan*, p. 379.
14. Yi Nŭnghwa 李能和, *Chosŏn togyosa* 朝鮮道敎史 (Yi Chongŭn tr., Seoul: 1982)

own revered priests.[15] Nevertheless, it had a profound and penetrating influence on Korean literature. Many Korean tales of wonder owe their existence to the influence of *Hsien* Taoism. Korean Taoist tradition held that the Samshin Mountains (The Three Sacred Mountains or Three Isles of the Blessed), the most prominent isles of the Taoist paradise, might exist somewhere in Korea.[16] Writings concerning these beliefs are manifold. The records of Chosŏn dynasty Taoist scholars acknowledge the existence of the legend which held that the Three Isles were part of Korea, though they themselves did not believe this to be true.[17]

Concurrent with the neo-Taoist movement in China, there arose a movement having as its objective the pursuit of immortality.[18] This involved the perpetuation of the mortal body by means of rigorous yogic practices aimed at ensuring the transition to an immortal state, in which one would be forever free of ageing and death. The ingestion of drugs was considered important — sometimes herbal preparations, but for the most part alchemic "elixirs of life." Taoist alchemy is transmitted in the *Nei p'ien* (Inner chapters) of Ko Hung's (283-343) *Pao-p'u tzu* (The Master Who Embraces Simplicity). Both as preliminary and ancillary procedures, he recommends Taoist yoga. Feats of magic and wearing of charms also played an important role. From this time on, Taoist philosophy gradually assimilated indigenous cults and superstitions, absorbing much from Buddhism. Thus arose the so-called *Hsien* Taoism. Ancient Chinese magical practices and the Immortality Cult probably provided the roots of *Hsien* Taoism.[19] Taoist worship and belief in alchemy and sorcery reached their height in the Hsüan-ho (1119-1125) period of the Sung dynasty. After the Yüan (1280-1368) dynasty, during which Buddhism was the most popular religion, Taoism declined. By the

---

15. See also Ch'a Chuhwan車柱環, *Han'guk togyo sasang yŏn'gu* 韓國道教思想研究 (Seoul:1983), p. 12.
16. Yi Chunghwan李重煥, *T'aengniji* 擇里志, (*Han'guk myŏngjŏ taejŏn chip*, Seoul:1973), pp. 175-176.
17. Ch'a Ch'ŏllo 車天輅, *Osan Sŏllim ch'ogo* 五山說林草藁 (*Taedong yasŭng*), (photo-reprint of 1909 ed., published by Kojŏn Kanhaenghoe, [13 vols, Seoul: 1968]), *kwŏn* 5, vol. l, pp. 596-672.
18. With the fall of the Later Han dynasty in 220 AD, Confucianism as the official cult became discredited. Such a situation led to the arousal of major philosophical movements, such as *hsüan hüeh* (Kor. *hyŏnhak*, Dark Learning), *ch'ing-t'an* (Kor. *ch'ŏngdam*, pure talk) — called neo-Taoism in general. This new departure was made by free-thinking scholars who were opposed to corruption of the government and who turned their backs on impurity. They used "pure talk" in the form of philosophical debate to destroy Confucian metaphysics. They had begun with the study of the *Tao te ching* and *Chuang tzu*, modifying the ancient doctrines and incorporating them with the Confucian *I ching*. The outcome was called "dark learning," and it is best represented by Wang Pi (226-49); Ho Yen (d. 249); Kuo Hsiang (d. 312) and the Seven Sages of the Bamboo Grove.
19. Herrlee G. Creel, *What is Taoism?* (Chicago and London: 1970), pp. l-24.

sixteenth century however, it was again dominant and influential in the literary activity of the period.[20]

It is understandable that the people of the Sŏnjo period were attracted to *Hsien* Taoism. Not only the Chinese influence of the time, but also the strictly secular and unyielding Confucianism must have left desires for religious solace unsatisfied. As the country was then racked by both factionalism and open warfare, it may be that the resultant personal hardships made any form of escape from the harsh adversity of daily life a great release. Evidence of the impact of *Hsien* Taoism on the literature of "outsiders" is traceable through a few traditional sources, such as Hong Manjong's *Headong ijŏk;*[21] Yi Kyugyŏng's (1788-?) *Oju yŏnmun changjŏn san'go, kwŏn 39, Tojangnyu,*[22] as well as the collection of *Shihwa* (Poetry talks), such as *Shihwa wa mallok,*[23] the modern translation of traditional Korean poetry criticism and the collected works of Kim Shisŭp, Hŏ Nansorhŏn and Hŏ Kyun. Some particular poems of these writers, such as *Yusŏnsa* (Wandering Immortals), *Nŭnghŏsa* (Song of Reaching Skyland) and *Pohŏsa* (Song of a Walk in Skyland), illustrate their great interest in immortality and the immortals.

Shamanism as a Background for Korean *Hsien* Taoism

Shamanism, firmly entrenched in the Korean mind, provided an important element in Korean *Hsien* Taoism. Shamanism in Korea, called *Musok*, has been portrayed as the mother religion of the country, for its coming into Korea far antedates any of the great religions, such as Confucianism, Buddhism or Taoism. It has, of course, been modified profoundly by these more sophisticated religions and to some extent, the influence has been reciprocal. Shamanism has been enriched by its absorption of each and every supernatural element, including the spirit worship of Taoism and the mysticism of Buddhism. The belief in spirits is inveterate and it has survived in spite of all social change and religious fashions, probably with more vitality than any of the religions which tried to undermine it.[24] Even though it formed the foundation-stone for the religious behaviour of the Korean people, Shamanism has always been despised by the literati as being fit only for women and the ignorant. Yet one cannot avoid concatenating Nansŏrhŏn's constant imaginary journey between the corporeal world and that of the deities to the spirit journey of shamans.

---

20. Lu Hsün, *A Brief History of Chinese Fiction* (Peking: 1959), p. 198.
21. Hong Manjong, *op. cit*, vol. 1, pp 125-99.
22. Yi Kyugyŏng 李圭景, *Oju yŏnmun changjŏn san'go* 五州衍文長箋散稿 photo-reprint of Kojŏn Kanhaenghoe ed., 2 vols, (Seoul: Tongguk Munhwasa,1976), vol. 2, pp. 195-6.
23. *SHML.*
24. According to Kim T'aegon's survey, the distribution of *mu* (shaman) in Korea was about 100,000 as of 31 August 1966.

It is believed that Shamanism had its origins amongst the Mongolic peoples, with the source of the Korean stock being the Amur Valley in Siberia. The golden crowns worn by the Shilla kings were proven to be of the same styles as those of the Siberian Shaman.[25]

Covell remarks that:

> The Siberian shaman's ability to fly to heaven to commune with spirits was a very major part of his powers. ...This symbolic power to fly was incorporated into the golden crowns of Shilla, since most of the crowns are dominated by two golden wings. ...Most shamans performing in Korea today have some sort of bird feathers attached to their hats.[26]

Shamanism covers a wide spectrum, consisting essentially of its superstitions and ceremonies but including also a fundamental way of observing nature and the spirits—the animism of the primitive race. It seems that Nansŏrhŏn's belief in the supernatural, the miracle within nature, so deeply-rooted in the Korean mind, made her susceptible to the idea of *Hsien* Taoism; advocating that human frailty could conquer fate and surmount a mundane existence. The mystical search for immortality is strikingly evident in Nansŏrhŏn's writing.

Conclusion

The advent of the Chosŏn dynasty, although of obvious social and political importance, did not usher in immediate change in the field of literature. Rigid control imposed by the literati officials perpetuated the preceding dynasty's literary genres and styles which were set in the Confucian mould. The new political regime was totally committed to the neo-Confucianisation of the population, and it was thus contrary to its interest to allow any other religion or ideology to oppose its plan. This included any movement for literary change away from the accepted Confucian values.

Perhaps the advent of *han'gŭl*, the phonetic alphabet of Korea, early in the new dynasty, offered a favourable time for writers to emerge in a new poetic direction. However, political considerations inhibited the use of the new alphabet and *hanmun* remained the common means of literary expression. The enmeshment of Korea's social, political and educational systems with neo-Confucian ideology, together with the commonality of *hanmun* with China, was too strong a thread to break by direct confrontation.

The two violent purges of the literati, the *Muo Sahwa* and *Kapcha Sahwa*, were an inauspicious start to the sixteenth century. Moreover, writers

---

25. Chang Chugŭn 張籌根, "Han'guk ŭi musok." *Han'guk ŭi musok munhwa* 韓國의 巫俗文化 (Seoul: Kukche Munhwa Chaedan, 1974), p. 227.
26. Allen Carter Covell, *Ecstasy:Shamanism in Korea* (Seoul:Hollym International Corp., 1983), pp. 31-33.

were denied creativity by King Chungjong's decree for the revival of neo-Confucian studies to help restore morality. It was thus almost fifty years before scholars tried to end their literary sterility in a muted ventilation of their disillusionment with the Confucian literary values. Earlier, some reconciliation of the differences between the literary traditions had been attempted, stemming from the proposition of Pak Sun to adopt T'ang poetic traditions to replace those of Sung. Excessive stylisation and ambiguity of content at the expense of a natural expression of feeling was also criticised by Pak Sun. In spite of these efforts literature relapsed into didactic sterility by the middle of the sixteenth century.

The Sung influence on poetry, extending over two centuries, persisted until about the beginning of King Sŏnjo's reign, when poets showed a transfer of interest to T'ang poetry. It was indeed a positive shift to the T'ang styles which Pak Sun had advocated almost half a century earlier. The "Three T'ang Talents of Korea" was a small but vital group. This switch of interest must not, however, be considered in isolation nor must the continuing impact of the Ming domination of poetry and its influence, albeit indirectly, on the Korean literary world of the sixteenth century be dismissed lightly, for this was the period of the neo-classical movement in China, centred around the "Former and Latter Seven Masters," of whom the best known included Li Meng-yang (1472-1529, styled Hsien-chi), Ho Ching-ming (styled Chung-mei), Li P'ang-lung (1514-1570) and Wang Shih-chen (1526-1590, styled Yen-chou shan-jen), that held that poetic perfection was to be found in the works of the eighth-century High T'ang poets.

If the beginning of the transition in Korean literature can be attributed to any single event, it could be that it was the institution of the *chinsa* examination that caused poetry to become the dominant form of literary expression. The votaries of both the *Sajang* and *Sallim* schools were irreconcilably divided in respect of their literary and philosophical tenets. However, these differences were to some extent tempered by the Confucian code, which ruled the lives and thoughts of all Koreans. To reiterate: success in personal life meant closer ties with the Confucian orthodoxy, whereas failure or lack of opportunity brought about rebellious attitudes or a conversion of belief to other religions such as Buddhism or Taoism. Importantly, writers who deviated from the Confucian pattern gravitated towards a new literary tradition, which became known as the "Literature of the Outsiders." It was only natural that as most of the "outsiders" were from a socially-deprived class, their hostility towards the established bureaucracy and neo-Confucian ideology would be very pronounced.

The influence of *Hsien* Taoism on the "outsiders" had the effect of linking their poetry with that of the "Three T'ang Talents." Unlike the "Three T'ang Talents" however, the "outsiders" wrote poetry predominantly as an outlet for social protest, personal dissatisfaction and disillusionment. Nonetheless, the "outsiders" had the courage, in a rigid and often hostile environment, to challenge the social system and Confucian ethics, even though they were completely lacking in power to bring about any change.

III
Nansŏrhŏn's Writing

Part 1 Derivation of Text

It was not considered proper for a woman to write poetry, although it was regarded as an essential part of an educated man's social life. Women therefore rarely wrote poems. When they did however, the poems they wrote were shown only to their families before being destroyed, for fear of damaging the reputation of the lineage. It was because of this discrimination that their poems were seldom published or handed down to later generations. Likewise, most of Nansŏrhŏn's poems—said to have been so many that they filled her room—were burnt in accordance with her wishes.[1] Only some of the poems kept at her parent's home were preserved.

The extant edition of Nansŏrhŏn's collection bears the title of *Nansŏrche chip* on the title page and *Nansŏrhŏn chip* as its cover title. This edition has a postscript[2] by Nansŏrhŏn's brother, Hŏ Kyun and two prefaces,[3] one by Chu Chi-fan (fl.1595), a Chinese envoy from the Ming Court and the other by his deputy, Liang Yu-nien. These are the only existing records pertaining to the collection's bibliographical background, other than short biographical and bibliographical introductions included in Chinese traditional sources.[4] These Chinese traditional sources appear to have been derived from the aforementioned postscript and prefaces, as well as from mere assumption. In his postscript, Hŏ Kyun reveals how he collected his sister's surviving poems, for fear of losing them, and had woodcuts made of them. He then introduced her poems to a wider-circle of readers, from May 1608. Chu Chi-fan wrote his

---

1. See Hŏ Kyun's Epilogue in Nansŏrhŏn chip.
2. *Ibid.*
3. *Nansŏrhŏn chip, CYYMJ*, p. 3.
4. See pp. 107-109,112 below.

preface in May 1606 and Liang Yu-nien's preface was written in January 1607. Liang Yu-nien ends his preface conjecturally, expressing the hope that Chinese historians would add Nansŏrhŏn's work to the illustrious literature of the Ming dynasty, to be handed-down for many generations to come.

Though it is often alleged that Chu Chi-fan first published *Nansŏrche chip* in China in 1606, there is no evidence to prove this. It is true however that selections from her collection are included in traditional Chinese anthologies such as Ch'ien Ch'ien-i's (1582-1644) *Lieh ch'ao shih chi* and others.[5] Ch'ien Ch'ien-i, in his brief introduction to Nansŏrhŏn in his *Lieh ch'ao shih chi* records that Chu Chi-fan had brought Nansŏrhŏn's collection back with him and it was widely circulated. This statement, together with others he made about Nansŏrhŏn being widowed and ending her days as a Taoist nun seem to be without foundation, since there is overwhelming evidence to the contrary. At the end of his introduction, he does say, however, that the selection of Nansŏrhŏn's poems included in *Lieh ch'ao shih chi* were quoted from *Cha'o hsien shih hsüan*. According to his own work entitled *Chiang-yun lou shu-mu*,[6] *Ch'ao hsien shih hsüan* originated during the Wan-li period (1573-1619) when a Chinese reinforcement army was sent into Korea. The marshal Wu Ming-chi of Ts'eng-chi accompanied the army to P'yongyang and while there collected poems. He adds that Hŏ Kyun (whom he refers to as the foremost Korean literary man) wrote the postscript to his collection. *Ch'ao hsien shih hsüan*, was published in 1599, or thereabouts[7] during the Wan-li period. This inclusion of Nansŏrhŏn's poems in *Ch'ao hsien shih hsüan* is sufficiently convincing to denote it as the first publication in China of her work.

The extant edition of Nansŏrhŏn's collection is believed to be the 1692 edition[8] which was originally published in Tongnae magistracy. The first Korean edition of 1608 (?) did not survive. The 1692 printing plates had been used for innumerable copies and are said to have become so worn that the characters were unrecognizable. Several different manuscripts which were copied by her readers have come down to us. In 1913 an edition of Nansŏrhŏn's collection combined

---

5. Ch'ien Ch'ien-i 錢謙益, *Lieh ch'ao shih chi* 列朝詩集, on *Kuei chi* 閨集, 6. Chu Yi-tsun's 朱彝尊 (1629-1709) *Ming shih tsung* 明詩綜, *chüan* 95, pt. 2, 1705 ed. Wu Ming-chi's 吳明濟 *Ch'ao-hsien shih hsüan* 朝鮮詩選 is not included in Shang-hai t'u shu kuan 上海圖書館, *Chung kuo ts'ung shu tsung lu* 中國叢書綜錄 (Peking:1960-1963) and is considered to be lost. Chu-ko Yüan-sheng's 諸葛元聲 *Liang ch'ao p'ing jang lu* 兩朝平壤錄, photo-reprint, (Taipei: 1969), p. 387-88.

6. Ch'ien Ch'ien-i, *Chiang yün lou shu mu* 絳雲樓書目, *chüan* 3, 15b, (Peking: 1958), p. 148.

7. Pak Yŏngu 朴英雨, "Chun'guk e sogae toen Hŏ Kyun kwa Nansŏrhŏn" 中國에 紹介된 許筠 과 蘭雪軒. Ch'ŏn'gu Taehakkyo, *Kugŏ kungmunhak yŏn'gu*, no. 1, pp. 51, 56.

8. See Kim Tujong 金斗鍾, *Han'guk koinswoe kisulsa* 韓國古印刷技術史, pp. 296, 381.

with a collection of poems by Hŏ Kyŏngnan, styled Sosŏrhŏn,[9] entitled *Hŏ puin Nansŏrhŏn chip pu Kyŏngnan chip* on the title page and *Nansŏl Sosŏrhŏn chip* as its cover title, was published by Shinhaeŭmsa in a modern type-face.

The collection consists of 211 poems with 50 titles, 2 pieces of prose and one piece of rhyme-prose. There are 15 five-syllable *koshi* (old-style verse), 8 seven-syllable *koshi*; 8 five-syllable *yulshi* (regulated verse); 13 seven-syllable *yulshi*; 25 five-syllable *chŏlgu* (quatrains);[10] 142 seven-syllable *chŏlgu* and 1 *kobu* (rhyme-prose). There are a few other poems which are not included in her collection, but found in other sources such as Yi Sugwang's *Chibong yusŏl* and Hŏ Kyun's *Haksan ch'odam*. Two of her poems entitled, "Kibu kangsa toksŏ" (To My Husband Studying in the Kangsa Reading Hall)[11]and "Ch'aeryŏn kok" (The Song of Lotus Gatherers),[12] both seven-syllable *chŏlgu*, are included in *Chibong yusŏl*. There is one *sa* (lyric) entitled "Ŏgao" (Fisherman's Home)[13] in Hŏ Kyun's *Haksan ch'odam*.

There are two *kasa* written in *han'gŭl*—"Kyuwŏn'ga" (Song of Woman's Complaint) and "Pongsŏnhwa ka" (Song of Colouring Nails with Touch-me-not Balsam), which are supposedly written by Nansŏrhŏn. Originally "Pongsŏnhwa ka" was included in *Ch'ŏngil-dang chapshik*. Yi Pyŏnggi (1892–1968) considered the poem similar to Nansŏrhŏn's *hanshi* entitled "Yŏnji pongsŏnhwa ka" and treated it as Nansŏrhŏn's work. Since then, it has been tradition among scholars to attribute it to Nansŏrhŏn. Recently, however, such scholars as O Haein[14] and Kang Chŏngsŏp[15] have expressed doubt about this. O Haein argues that the two poems are only similar in title, and that one lacks Nansŏrhŏn's freshness of imagery, beauty of diction, and most of all the fantasy that pervades so much of her poetry. She points out that it is more like a ballad song composed for or by a singer purely for the purpose of entertainment. I support O Haein's standpoint. Chang Chin in her thesis entitled *Hŏ Nansŏrhŏn non*,[16] shares the same opinion.

---

9. Hŏ Kyŏngnan 許景蘭, a poetess of the Ming dynasty was a daughter of Hŏ Sun 許巡, a Korean Translating Officer posted to the Ming Court during the reign of King Sŏnjo, by his Chinese wife. Her style Sosŏrhŏn was taken out of her respect for Hŏ Nansŏrhŏn. Poems in her collection are written to the tunes of Nansŏrhŏn's poems.

10. Some of these quatrains may be treated as *akpu* songs. See chapter III, part 4 below.

11. Yi Sugwang, *op. cit.*, pp. 256-257.

12. *Ibid.*

13. *HKCS*, p. 464.

14. *NSC*, p. 353.

15. Kang Chŏnsŏp 姜銓燮, "*Moktongga ŭi pogwŏn e taehayŏ*". Paekkang Sŏ Susaeng Paksa Hwan'gap Kinyŏm Nonch'ong Kanhaeng Wiwŏnhoe, *Han'guk shiga yŏu'gu* 韓國詩歌硏究 (Seoul:1981), p. 332.

16. Chang Chin 張眞, *Hŏ Nansŏrhŏn non* 許蘭雪軒論, An M.A. thesis submitted to Tongguk Taechakkyo (Seoul:1980), p. 282.

_____, *Hŏ Nansŏrhŏn non* 許蘭雪軒論, *Tongak ŏmun nonjip* 東岳語文論集, vol. 12, 1980.

"Kyuwŏn'ga" is included in the *Kogŭm kagok* as written by Nansŏrhŏn. There is a *kasa* called "Wŏnbusa" (Song of Woman's Complaint)[17] written by Muok, mistress of Hŏ Kyun, of which only the title has come down to us and some scholars argue that the "Kyuwŏn'ga" by Nansŏrhŏn may well be Muok's "Wŏnbuga." In view of the likelihood that these two *kasa* are not, in fact, Nansŏrhŏn's work, they have been excluded from further discussion.

Part 2 Study of Her Poetic Thought

In theme and content Nansŏrhŏn's poems are indisputably lacking in inventiveness. The fact that some two-thirds are in *akpu* style could be the main reason for this, for they are the reworking of traditional themes drawn from early Chinese folksongs. Also, like the T'ang poets who wrote *akpu*-style poems (called new *yüeh-fu* or imitation folksongs), she adopted the themes of the early ballads to express her feelings, as well as the lively idioms in which they were cast. She frequently copied the titles of some older *akpu* which unlike *sa* did not follow a fixed melodic pattern. Nansŏrhŏn's models can be traced to the Wei (220-265) and Chin (265-420) dynasties in China. During these periods, poets such as Ts'ao Chih (192-232) and Lu Chi (261–303) wrote excellent *akpu*. Nansŏrhŏn's poems often have the titles of old *akpu* songs, leading the reader to doubt their authenticity.[18]

Nevertheless, Nansŏrhŏn developed an indigenous style of conspicuous simplicity and sincerity. This is reputed to be as pure and graceful as Koryŏ porcelain, with a lively diction reinforced by a vivid imagination. Although her education and upbringing were prescribed by strict neo-Confucian orthodoxy, she drew her spiritual inspiration more from Taoism or humanism. Throughout her life she suffered the mental turmoil of two conflicting emotions. One was centred on the expected role of a wife and daughter-in-law of a *yangban* family in the rigid Chosŏn society. The other was the enduring wish to break through the social barriers which prevented her from becoming a carefree, happy person. The latter would, of course, have included the liberty to write poetry unfettered by the shackles which confined women to the domestic realm. Her verses express this conflict; she was unable to find an outlet for her ambition, talent and good education. As the years passed, her insoluble anguish deepened and she turned to the occult world of the immortals for consolation. A strong belief in immortality is expressed repeatedly in her poems, with some explicit descriptions of her visions. The following provide good examples:

---

17. Hong Manjong, *Sunoji*. Hong Manjong *op. cit.*, vol. 1, p. 94.

Wandering Immortals

Poem 14

At leisure, with my two young sisters,
I go to pay my respects in Heaven;[19]
Immortals[20] of the Three Islands[21] call to see us.
I command the Scarlet Dragon[22] to be harnessed
    amidst the flowers;
At the Purple Emperor's palace we watch the Dart and Bottle
    game.[23]

---

18. For a fuller discussion of this point see Chapter IV below.

19. Hsüan Tu (Kor. Hyŏndo) 玄都 "Abstruse Land" is the name of the cave of Lao tzu in the *Feng shen yen i* 封神演義. In chap. 44 it records, Ch'ih Ching Tzu (Kor. Chŏkchŏng-ja) 赤精子 rode on fair clouds bound for the Abstruse Land and in an instant he arrived at this fairy mountain. It was the Cave of the Abstruse Land, Hsüan-tu Tung (Kor. Hyŏndo Dong) 玄都洞 of the Ta-lo (Kor. Taera) Palace 大羅宮 where Lao tzu resided and within it there was the Pa Ching (Kor. P'algyŏng) Palace or "Palace of Eight-scenes". The name Hsüan Tu has very early origins, and since the sixth century has been adopted as the name of a Taoist monastery.—*Han Wu-ti nei chuan.* See Liu Ts'un-yen, *op. cit.*, p. 137.

20. Chen jen (Kor. chinin) 眞人 "Perfected beings or Immortals." The second class deified mortals, the first class being Chen chün 眞君 "Immortal master." See *Sung shi* 宋史, Chap. 105, *Li Chih* 禮志, 8.

21. The Three Isles or Three Mountains, described as being in the shape of three gourds are in the Eastern Sea. The first one is the Fang-hu (Kor. Pangho) 方壺 or the Fang-chang (Kor. Pangjang) 方丈 Hill; the second is the P'eng-hu (Kor. Pongho) 蓬壺 or the P'eng-lai Hill; and the third is the Ying-hu (Yŏngho) 瀛壺 or the Ying-chou (Kor. Yŏngju) 瀛州 Hill.—Wang Chia, *Shih i chi, chüan* 1, *Ku-chin i-shih* ed. See also *Shih chi, chüan* 28.

22. Ch'ih lung (Kor. Chŏgyong) 赤龍: in Li Ho's death-bed vision a man dressed in dark red, in a carriage drawn by the scarlet dragon, appears to escort Li Ho to heaven where the heavenly Emperor has completed the White Jade Tower and summons him to compose the inscription. See Li Shang-yin, *Li I-shan wen chi* 李義山文集, *Ssu-pu ts'ung-k'an* ed. vol. IV, p. 21a.

23. Ancient game of pitching arrows into a pot—the loser has to drink a forfeit.

Stirred by My Experience

Poem 4

At night in dream I climbed Mt. Pongnae,[24]
My feet on the dragon of Ko-p'o bank.[25]
An immortal with a magic bamboo cane
Invited me to Lotus Hill.
I looked down on the Eastern Sea,[26]
As tranquil as a cup of water.
Beneath the lotuses a phoenix played the flute;
The moon shone on the golden jar.

Neo-Taoist influence strongly pervades her work. Nansŏrhŏn constantly dreamed of being able to divest herself of worldly fetters and fly beyond the stifling world, where everything seemed to be wrong for her, to the realm of the Immortals. She lamented that she had not been born a man, nor blessed with a happy marriage. Thus the fact that so many poems in her collected works are devoted to immortality comes as no surprise. These poems include visions of nature deities and immortals of the Taoist lore. Perhaps her tutor, Yi Tal, together with her family of scholars, influenced her in the desperate wish to find some substitute for the world around her. It would, of course, be remiss not to mention here the great influence on Nansŏrhŏn of such poets as Li Po (705-762), Li Ho (790-816) and Li Shang-yin (813-858) of the T'ang dynasty. The quest for immortality touched Nansŏrhŏn, as it did many Koreans, with the cult's greatest influence being felt between the reigns of King Chungjong (1506-44) and King Sŏnjo,[27] the period during which most of her poems were written.

---

24. P'eng-lai (shan) 蓬萊山: Among the large number of lesser Paradises of the Taoists Hai-chung San shan (Kor. Haejung Samsan) 海中三山 "The Three Isles or Three Hills in the (Eastern) Sea" stand out prominently. Of these P'eng-lai shan (Kor. Pongnae san) is the most famous. The houses are made of gold and silver. The birds and animals are all white. The pearl and coral trees grow there in great profusion. The flowers and seeds all have a sweet flavour. Those who eat them do not grow old nor die. There they drink of the fountain of life, and live in ease and pleasure. The Isles are surrounded with water which has no buoyancy, so it is impossible to approach them. They are inhabited only by the immortals, who have supernatural powers of transpotation. These islands are the goal of many earnest Taoists.—Wang Chia 王嘉, *Shih i chi* 拾遺記. *Chüan* 1 and *Chüan* 10, *Ku-chin i-shih* ed.

25. *Kop'o lung* (Kor. *Kalp'i yong*) 葛陂龍: Fei Ch'ang-fang 費長房, who studied magic with Hu-weng 壺翁 "Lord Pot," was given by the latter a *lu yü chang* (Kor. *nogokchang*) 綠玉杖 "a bamboo cane" on which one could ride. When Fei Ch'ang-fang threw his cane into the Ko-p'o bank in Honan Province, it turned into a dragon. see *Hou Han shu* 後漢書. *Chüan* 82, Chung-hua shu chü ed.

26. The Eastern Isles were said to be in the Eastern Sea off the coast of China; see *Shih chi* 史記, *chüan* 6, Chung hua shu chü ed.

27. See p. 24-25 above.

Another major influence on Nanŏrhŏn's poetic style was *Ch'u tz'u*. Professor David Hawkes divides the majority of the *Ch'u tz'u* into two main categories: *tristia* and *itineraria*. The *Ch'u-tz'u* tradition, which fascinated such T'ang poets as Li Po, Li Ho and Li Shang-yin, also directly inspired Nansŏrhŏn's poems. The following versions of the poem, "Song of the Magic String" (which describes shaman exorcism) as written by Li Ho and Nansŏrhŏn, provide us with an example. Both reveal the influence of the *Ch'u tz'u* tradition.

Li Ho:

As the sun sets in the western hills
The eastern hills grow dark.
A whirlwind blows the horses along,
Steeds trampling the clouds.
Painted zithers and plain flutes
Play soft, weird tunes.
To the rustle of embroidered skirts
She treads the autumn dust.

Cassia leaves stripped by the wind,
Cassia seeds fall,
Blue racoons are weeping blood
As shivering foxes die.
On the ancient wall are painted dragons,
Tails inlaid with gold,
Rain-elves are riding them away
To the autumn tarn.
Owls that have lived a hundred years,
Turned forest demons,
Find emerald fire, laughing wildly,
Leap from their nests. [28]

Nansŏrhŏn:

Banana flowers weep dew at the bend of the River Hsiang;
Over the nine peaks[29] an autumn mist, the sky fringed with
    green.

---

28. See J.D. Frodsham, *The Poems of Li Ho* (Oxford: 1970), p. 212.
29. Nine peaks of Mt. Chiu-i 九疑山, also called Mt. Ts'ang-wu where Emperor Shun is reputed to be buried, is in the present Ning-yüan county, Hunan Province. See *Han shu* 漢書, *chüan* 6, Chung hua shu chü ed.

In the underwater palace[30] the waves are chill and dragons[31]
　　roar at night;
A Southern girl touched by grief is like elegant jade.
The male phoenix has flown away to distant Mt. Ts'ang-wu;[32]
The rain-filled air shrouds the river, dimming the dawn light.
At leisure, high on the cliff, she plucks the magic strings;
With tresses of flowers and moonlight the Hsiang beauties
　　weep.
In a sky of jade, the distant ramparts of the Milky Way.
Parasols with golden shafts drown in multi-coloured clouds.
Outside the gate fishermen sing the Bamboo Branch song;[33]
Over a silvery lake the moon of longing lovers droops
　　halfway.

The eighty-seven *Yusŏnsa* (Wandering Immortals) poems, as well as
much of Nansŏrhŏn's other writing contain descriptions of nature, especially
of travels in mountainous regions, but then launch into the visionary realm of
nature deities and immortals. She ranges freely between the corporeal world
and the visionary realm she shared with the poets of the *Ch'u tzu*. These
poems had a common theme and very old theme—that of the virtuous man,
disillusioned with his life, who tries to become a hermit or an immortal.
According to Stephen Owen, the theme had its beginnings in the Ch'un-ch'iu
period, with the legends of ancient hermits who refused to serve the state.

　　Nansŏrhŏn's immersion in these themes appears to be deeper than that
of her Chinese counterparts. The reason for this may be that Shamanism had
deep roots in the indigenous mind, and provided an important bedrock for
Korean neo-Taoism; far more ancient than any other religion, it survived all
social change and foreign cultural influence. Nansŏrhŏn's mystical faith was
twofold: belief in the supernatural, and in the cosmic flight of the human

---

30. Shui fu (Kor. Subu) 水府 is the Treasury or Palace of Waters. There are four main divisions
of the Palace in which the Dragon-saint is the president of the Supreme Council and the Dragon-
kings of the Four Seas form the Body of Four Ministers. See *DCM*, p. 433.
31. *Ibid.*
32. See n. 36, p. 38 below.
33. *Chu chih tz'u* (Kor. *Chukchi-sa*) 竹枝詞 "Song of the Bamboo Branches": an *akpu* song
which originated from the Yangtze valley. There are two theories on the derivation of this ballad:
(a) Liu Yu-hsi, when he visited Chien-an 建安, heard a folksong, called *chu-chih* 竹枝, being
sung by children which is said to have adapted as a love song.
(b) While Liu Yu-hsi was in Yüan-shang 沅湘, in the South he came across this folksong, which
he thought to be rather crude, and rewrote it according to the *Chiu ko* of *Ch'u tz'u* tradition. The
reason that it is called *Chu-chih* alludes to the practice of whipping bamboo canes at their ritual
ceremony. See *YFSC*, *Ch'in-tai ch'ü tz'u*, Chapter 81.

mind. Poetic inspiration brought vivid descriptions of her dreams and visions. The Taoist heaven recurs constantly in her poems as a place of exquisite beauty and the dwelling place of immortals.

Her *Yusŏnsa* poems display a far stronger belief in immortality than was apparently held by any of the T'ang poets who supposedly influenced her. This is supported by the fact that her *yusŏnsa* poems are much more numerous than their Chinese counterparts and their descriptions are much deeper and more explicit. Nansŏrhŏn describes the Taoist heaven as a real place; like-wise, her poetry never doubts the existence of immortals. Her theme of the disappointed person, who seeks either immortality or the solitary isolation of the hermit, prompts her to reveal her own disillusionment, as well as that of women generally, in the rigid and stereotyped Chosŏn society. It may well be that she attempted to gain immortality for herself by any means available, such as the consumption of elixir or the practice of Taoist yoga. Her poem, "On Chasing Away Sad Thoughts" which indicates a search for the elusive elixir, reads:

Poem 8

> Fragrant trees flourish with fresh greenery;
> Nutmeg leaves already sprout everywhere.
>
> In Spring, nature turns to elegant beauty;
> But I alone am full of sadness and grief.
>
> On my wall, a map of the Five Sacred Mountains;[34]
> At the table head is the *Ts'an t'ung ch'i*;[35]
> If my quest for the elixir succeeds,
> I will pay homage to Emperor Shun.[36]

In most of her immortality poems, however, Nansŏrhŏn projects herself either as a visitor to the immortal world or as someone who is already there, rather than as a person who simply admires and earnestly yearns for it. A story relates that Nansŏrhŏn used to wear the corolla of a flower when she recited her poems,[37] many of which would seem to be records of unfeigned visions in

34. *Wu yo* 五嶽 (Kor. *Oak*). The Five Sacred Mountains. North: Heng Shan, in Shansi; South: Heng Shan, in Hunan; East: T'ai Shan, in Shantung; West: Hua Shan, in Shensi; Centre: Sung Shan, in Honan. See *DCM*, pp. 578-579.

35. *Ts'an t'ung ch'i* (Kor. *Ch'amdonggye*) 參同契, a book compiled about 140 A.D. by Wei Po-yang 魏白陽 is the oldest surviving text on Taoist alchemy. Kwŏn Kŭkchung wrote *Ch'amdonggye chuhae* 參同契註解.

36. Yü Shun 虞舜, the Emperor Shun, the legendary Chinese ruler said to have been buried in Mt. Ts'ang-wu 蒼梧.

37. Ch'a Sangch'an 車相瓚, "Hŏ Nansŏrhŏn," *Pando sahwa wa nakt'o Manju* 半島史話와樂土滿洲, (1942).

which she rose above the earthly world. A poem from *Yusŏnsa* (Wandering Immortals) is germane here:

Poem 87

> A skirt with six strips of brocade trail along the clouds,
> She calls young Juan[38] and ascends to the iris fields;
> Suddenly the lute music among the flowers stops;
> In the temporal world ten thousand years have passed.

Although some commentators are inclined to describe Nansŏrhŏn as a woman who spent her whole life bemoaning her sad fate, and constantly trying to escape into another world, there is proof that this was not in fact so. Some of her poems show clearly that she was interested in things other than the seemingly incessant quest for mystical bliss. It is evident that she felt deep concern for contemporary affairs and an unbearable sadness in the face of the injustice and misery she saw about her, as instanced by her poem, "The Poor Girl":

Poems 1, 4, 3.

> Surely she does not lack beauty
> Nor skills in sewing and weaving.
> But she grew up in a poor family
> So good matchmakers ignore her.
>
> She never looks cold or hungry,
> All day long she weaves by the window.
> Only her parents feel sorry for her;
> Neighbours would never know of it.
>
> A pair of golden scissors in her hand,
> Fingers stiffened by the night's chill.
> She cuts a bridal costume for another,
> Yet year after year she sleeps alone.

At times, her poems refer explicitly to relatives, such as the parting from her brother or husband, the death of her children and other family affairs. These provide useful information for her biography. Unfortunately, such references are few. Her major poems are for the most part about dreams and are seldom informative as to the times and circumstances in which they were written. Even her two pieces of prose, which might have provided some further biographical information, both describe journeys to the spiritual world.

---

38. Juan Chao 阮肇 of the Later Han dynasty (25-220). Legend has it that Juan Chao, together with Liu Ch'en went into the mountains to gather herbs, where they met the goddess and became immortal. See *Shang yu lu* 尚友錄, *chüan* 15.

A final characteristic of Nansŏrhŏn's poetry is its highly melancholic content, even by accepted Korean and Chinese standards. This tendency is not, however, as peculiar to her poetry as many present-day Korean scholars seem to suggest. A tone of melancholy was introduced into Chinese literature by the *Ch'u tz'u* poems, and was much admired and appreciated. Lines from such poems as *Ku-shih shih-chiu shou* (Nineteen Old Poems) illustrate this:

> Northwest the tall tower stands,
> Its top level with floating clouds,
> Patterned windows webbed in lattice,
> Roofs piled three stories high.
> From above, the sound of strings and song;
> What sadness in that melody!
> Who could play a tune like this,
> Who but the wife of Ch'i Liang[39]

> The clear shang[40] mode drifts down the wind;
> Halfway through, it falters and breaks, one plucking,
> Two of three sighs, longing, a grief that lingers on -
> It is not the singer's pain I pity,
> But few are those who understand the song!
> If only we could be a pair of calling cranes,
> Beating wings, soaring to the sky! [41]

This plaintive mood prevailed in nearly all the poetry of late T'ang and the succeeding Five Dynasties. Nansŏrhŏn's verse plumbs the very depths of pessimism. Many scholars describe her poems as profoundly melancholic, with sorrow as their prevailing quality. In addition to the general influence of T'ang verse, there were other reasons for her pessimism—the tragic death of both of her children before they reached adulthood, her feeling of having failed as a wife and daughter-in-law, as well as a constant and fearful awareness of the unstable political situation. Political factions were a direct threat to the central government, and a potential danger to members of her

---

39. Ch'i Liang, a man of the state of Ch'i, was killed in battle in 550 B.C.E. According to legend, his grief-stricken wife committed suicide by throwing herself into the Tzu River, Burton Watson, *Chinese Lyricism*, p. 25.

40. Shang is one of the five modes or keys of traditional Chinese music, that associated with autumn, hence the epithet "clear." The association with autumn also suggests sadness and decay, Burton Watson, *op. cit.*, p. 25.

41. The above translation and its notes are from Burton Watson, *op. cit.*, p. 25. See Hsiao T'ung 蕭統 (501-531), *Wen hsüan* 文選, *chüan* 29, (Peking, 1974 reprint), vol. 10, for original text.

family, who were leading members of the party opposing the regime of the day. Naturally, she dreaded her family's eventual downfall.

Many of Nansŏrhŏn's melancholic poems have, for their subject, the neglected woman, possibly a record of Nansŏrhŏn's own experience. They are mostly cast in the mold of the *akpu* tradition. Variously termed as *ae* 哀, *wŏn* 怨 or *pi* 悲, a court code of poetic convention, governing subject, theme, mood and attitude sets the prevailing sad tone of Nansŏrhŏn's poetry. An interesting statistical analysis of Nansŏrhŏn's verse records thirty-five separate expressions of sadness and eleven of anxiety.[42] Taking into account that some two-thirds of Nansŏrhŏn's poems are dedicated to the world of the immortals, free from sorrow and anxiety, the remaining one-third display this unhappy burden. Inevitably, we must conclude that all her poems about worldly things are concerned with unhappiness or sadness in one way or another. Accordingly, it is no wonder that many scholars have labeled her poetry as predominantly melancholic with sorrow as its dominant quality. Two-thirds of her poems are neo-Taoist in theme and these require a great deal of annotation because of her profuse Taoist allusions.

Part 3 Nansŏrhŏn's Poetic Form

Nansŏrhŏn used all the ordinary verse forms in which the T'ang poets wrote: *koshi* and *kŭnch'eshi* including *chŏlgu* and *yulshi,* though she showed a strong preference for *kŭnch'eshi*, especially for *chŏlgu* which is the most concentrated form of *hanshi* or Chinese poetic form and as such requires the greatest economy of words. Of the 214 extant poems in her collected works, 23 are written in *koshi* form; 21 in *yulshi*; 169 in *chŏlgu* and 1 in *sa*.[43] She has a great fondness for compressed, highly polished language. Most of her poems are *akpu* (*yüeh-fu*) style in theme and content, drawn from the old themes of Chinese folk-songs, but into which she infuses a highly individual Korean imagination, with a simple and lively diction.

Nansŏrhŏn composed many *akpu* in this category, mostly of the five and seven syllable *chŏlgu* with its great economy of words. In her collection the poems are grouped under poetic form headings, while her *akpu* songs are grouped under the respective forms in which her ballads are cast. My own analysis of her seventy poems has shown that some verses are grouped under the wrong headings, and this has been pointed out in the commentary to individual poems. There would seem to be a simple reason why the *akpu* form was not included in her collection as a distinct heading.

---

42. Kim Yongsuk, *Chosŏn yŏryu munhak ŭi yŏn'gu* (Seoul: 1979), pp. 361-78.
43. Some classifications of her poems in her collected work, proved to be wrong. Thus the number quoted here may vary slightly.

In fact, all of her five-syllable and seven-syllable *chŏlgu* and most of her old-style verses are *akpu* ballads, at least in title and content. Furthermore, several of her poems which have been assigned to a miscellaneous grouping, when analysed show some common phenomena of poetic structure and turn out to be *akpu*, written in five-syllable and seven syllable *chŏlgu*. For these reasons, the original editor must have grouped her poems under the headings of line forms, even though her works resemble a collection of *akpu*. Thus, it could be said that except for a mere handful of poems about her private life, she wrote only *akpu* style poems. Table "A" illustrates the possible origin of Nansŏrhŏn's *akpu*. The*Yüeh-fu shih chi* and its supplement by Masuda Kiyohide, are used here, as authoritative reference. *Yüeh-fu shih chi* is the main repository of *akpu* poetry, and includes almost all extant examples from the end of the third century B.C.E. down to the tenth century C.E. The *akpu* poetry in this repository is classified under 12 different categories and these classifying headings convey the information about origin and background of the songs.

Table A

Traditional *akpu* titles found in her collection	Number of her poems	Possible models for Nansŏrhŏn's *akpu* found in *YFSC* under Kuo's classifying headings
1. *Sonyŏn haeng* 小年行 "Song of Youth"	1	*Ts'a-ch'i ko tz'u* (Kor. *chapkok kasa*) "Miscellaneous songs"(*chüan.* 61-78) *chüan.* 66.
2. *Ch'ulsae kok* 出塞曲 "Leaving the Pass"	2	*H'eng-ch'ui ch'u tz'u* "Songs accompanied by horizontal flutes" (*chüan.* 21-25).
3. *Maksu ak* 莫愁樂 "Free from Care"	2	*Chieng-shang ch'u-tz'u* "Songs in the tunes *ch'ing* and *shang* (*chüan.* 44-51), *chüan.* 48.
4. *Pinnyŏ ŭm* 貧女吟 "Song for the Poor Girl"	4	New, *Yüeh-fu* poems (*chüan.* 90-100), *chüan.* 96.
5. *Hyo Ts'ui Kuo-fu ch'e* 效崔國輔體 "Imitation of Ts'ui Kuo-fu's style"	3	Matching songs (*chüan.* 26-43), *chüan.* 42.
6. *Changgan haeng* 長干行 "Song of Chang-kan" or "The River Merchant's Wife"	2	Miscellaneous songs (*chüan.* 61-78), *chüan.* 72.
7. *Kangnam kok* 江南曲 "Song of the Land South of the River"	5	*Hsiang-ho ko tz'u* "Matching songs" (*chüan.* 26-43), *chüan.* 26.
8. *Kogaek sa* 賈客詞 "Song of the Merchants"	3	Songs in the tunes *ch'ing* and *shang* (ch. 44-51), *chüan.* 48

9.	*Sangbong haeng* 相逢行 "On the City Street"	2	Matching songs (*chüan.* 26-43), *chüan.* 34.
10.	*Taeje kok* 大堤曲 "Great Dyke"	2	Songs in the tunes *ch'ing* and *shang* (*chüan.* 44-51), *chüan.* 48.
11.	*Pohŏ sa* 步虛詞 "Song of a Walk in Skyland"	2	Miscellaneous songs (*chüan.* 61-78), *chüan.* 78.
12.	*Ch'ŏngnu kok* 靑樓曲 "Courtesan's song"	1	New, *Yüeh-fu* poems (*chüan.* 90-100), *chüan.* 91.
13.	*Saeha kok* 寒下曲 "Beyond the Frontier"	5	Hsin yüeh-fu tz'u, "New *yüeh-fu* poems" (*chüan.* 90-100), *chüan.* 92.
14.	*Ipsae kok* 入塞曲 "Entering the Pass"	5	Songs accompanied by horizontal flutes (*chüan.* 21-25) *chüan.* 22.
15.	*Chukchi sa* 竹枝詞 "Song of Bamboo Branches"	4	Ch'in-tai ch'u tz'u "Songs of recent times" (*chüan.* 79- 82), *chüan.* 81.
16.	*Chesang haeng* 提上行 "By the Dyke"	1	New *yüeh-fu* poems (*chüan.* 90-100), *chüan.* 94.
17.	*Kung sa* 宮詞 "Palace Songs"	20	Matching songs (*chüan.* 26-43), *chüan.* 43.
18.	*Yangyuji sa* 楊柳枝詞 "Song of Willow Branches"	5	Songs of recent times (*chüan.* 79- 81), *chüan.* 81.
19.	*Yusŏn sa* 遊仙詞 "Wandering Immortals"	87	Matching songs (*chüan.* 26-43), *chüan.* 37.
20.	*Yajwa* 夜坐(吟) "Sitting through the Night"	1	Miscellaneous songs (*chüan.* 61-78), *chüan.* 76.
21.	*Kyuwŏn* 閨怨 "A Woman's grievance"	2	Matching songs (*chüan.* 26-43), *chüan.* 42.
22.	*Ch'uhan* 秋恨 "Autumn plaint"	1	Matching songs (*chüan.* 26-43), *chüan.* 42.
23.	*Ch'aeryŏn kok* 采蓮曲 "Song of Lotus Gatherers"	1	Songs in the tunes *ch'ing* and *shang* (*chüan.* 44-51), *chüan.* 50. Total 161

Part 4 Translations with Notes and Commentaries

Ideally, the presentation of Nansŏrhŏn's work here should be chronological, taking into consideration her natural development as a poetess as well as any changes in attitude resulting from age and experience. However, because of the lack of biographical data, it has been possible to date only one of her poems. It is for this reason, with a few exceptions, that I have arranged my translations and commentaries in accordance with the order in which the poems appear in her collected works, *Nansŏrhŏn chip*[44] (See Table B on p. 45 for arrangement of translated poems and prose in the book).

Translations and interpretations of fifty three of Nansŏrhŏn's poems are presented. The poems selected are representative of each thematic or stylistic group, as well as being those which fit better into English. Poems which provide some background about her personal life have been given priority. Special attention has been paid to the formal and non-formal structures, taking into consideration sound, syntax and meaning. In regard to the phonetic features, each character has been checked against a tonal table to define the tone of each rhyme and the tonal pattern of each verse.

I have attempted a compromise between literal and literary translation. The division of a poem into lines and stanzas has been kept intact, with the exception that some 7-syllable lines are divided into two lines by breaking at the caesura. Minimal change has been made to the word order. Wherever possible, I have tried to convey parallelism and antithesis as in the original text although I have not attempted to reproduce line length, rhyme and tonal balance.

All the translations are my own, though most of the notes are taken from various Chinese traditional sources. Whenever English translations of the relevant sources are available I have quoted such translations themselves instead of attempting to retranslate originals. Translations however have always been checked against the original source. The originals of the poems translated are also presented. Charts which indicate the tone of rhymes and tonal patterns of each verse are provided at the head of the translation, next to the original text. In each chart, "O" represents the level tone; "X" the deflected tone; "@" rhyme in level tone and "*" rhyme in deflected tone.

---

44. See *Nansŏrhŏn chip, CYYMJ*, pp. 3-23.

Table B

Arrangement of Translated Poems and Prose in the Book

Original text	Translation		Page
	5-syllable koshi		
1	1	Song of Youth (小年行)	46
2	2	Stirred by My Experience (感遇), poems 3 and 4	48
3	3	Mourning for My Children (哭子)	50
4	4	On Chasing Away Sad Thoughts (遣興), poems 5 and 8	52
5	5	To Hagok (寄荷谷)	54
	7-syllable koshi		
7	6	Colouring Nails with Touch-me-not Balsam (染指鳳仙花歌)	55
9	7	Song of the Magic Strings by the Hsiang River (湘絃謠)	57
10	8	Poems for the Four Seasons (四時詞), poem 1, Spring and poem 2, Summer	59
	5-syllable chŏlgu		
26	9	Song of Free from Care (莫愁樂), 2 poems	63
27	10	Song for the Poor Girl (貧女吟), 4 poems	65
28	11	Imitation of Ts'ui Kuo-fu's Style (效崔國輔體)	67
29	12	Song of Ch'ang-kan (長干行), 2 poems	69
30	13	Song of the Land South of the River (江南曲), 5 poems	71
	7-syllable chŏlgu		
34	14	Song of a Walk in Skyland (步虛詞), 1 poem	75
35	15	Courtesan's Song (青樓曲), 1 poem	77
41	16	Swing Song (鞦韆詞), 2 poems	78
42	17	Palace Song (宮詞), 9 poems	79
46	18	Wandering Immortals (遊仙詞), 8 poems	85
48	19	A Woman's Grievance (閨怨), 2 poems	91
49	20	Autumn Plaint (秋恨)	93
	Miscellaneous		
	(for classification see each work in the book)		
52 (prose 2)			
	21	Roaming Mount Kwangsang in a Dream: Preface and poem (夢遊廣桑上詩兼序)	94
	From other sources		
From CBYS			
	22	To My Husband Studying in the Kangsa Hall of Reading (寄夫江舍讀書)	98
From CBYS			
	23	Song of Lotus Gatherers (采蓮曲)	100

Translation 1

"Song of Youth"

Form: *Koshi*

Rhyme Pattern
word no. 1 2 3 4 5
line no.

少	年	重	然	諾		
結	交	遊	俠	人	2	@
腰	間	玉	轆	轤		
錦	袍	雙	麒	麟	4	@
朝	辭	明	光	宮		
馳	馬	長	樂	阪	6	*
沽	得	渭	城	酒		
花	間	日	將	晚	8	*
金	鞭	宿	倡	家		
行	樂	爭	留	連	10	@
誰	憐	揚	子	雲		
閉	門	草	太	玄	12	@

A young man true to his promise
Joins the wandering folk heroes.
At his waist, a jade sword,
Robe embroidered with two unicorns.[45]
Bidding farewell to the court at Ming-kuang Palace, [46]
He gallops his horse down Ch'ang-lo slope,
And goes to buy wine of Wei-ch'eng[47]
Among the flowers;[48] day draws toward evening.
With his golden whip, he spends all night in the brothels,
Seeking to pass the time in search of pleasure.

---

45. One of the Four Spiritual Animals:*In* (Ch. *Lin* 麟, unicorn), *Pong* (Ch.*Feng* 鳳, Phoenix), *Ku* (Ch. *Kuei* 龜, Tortoise) and *Yong* (Ch. *Lung* 龍, the Dragon).
46. One of the palaces of Han dynasty, which was built by the Emperor Wu. See *Han shu, chüan* 6, *Wu-ti Chi* 武帝記, Chung hua shu chü ed.
47. A famous wine. The modern location is just to the northeast of Hsien-yang, in Shan-hsi.
48. A reference to beautiful women or courtesans.

> Who would pity Yang Hsiung,[49]
> Staying at home, drafting the *T'ai hsüan ching*.[50]

Commentary

Kuo Mao-ch'ien's *YFSC* includes approximately 63 of the *akpu* ballads with the "bravo" or "knight-errant" theme in *chüan* 66. Cheng Chiao's (1104-1162) *T'ung-chih*,[51] also contains 21 ballads of the same theme of Han, Wei, Six Dynasties and T'ang period under such titles as "Pacts with Friends on the Sporting Fields of Youth," "Ch'ang-an Bravos," "Song of Youth" etc., in *chüan* 49.

Some ballads on the bravo theme tended to emphasise the failure of bravos, whereas others give prominence to heroism and gallantry. This poem by Nansŏrhŏn follows the latter emphasis in the first three couplets, and then in the middle reveals her increasing disdain, finally sneering at the hypocrisy of the gallantry theme in her last three couplets.

The poem is a 5-syllable *koshi* which changes its rhyme during the course of the poem at the end of each couplet: level tone at the first couplet, deflected tone at the second, and then back to the level tone at the third. This is one of the characteristics of *koshi* which distinguishes it from *Kŭnch'e shi*. There is a caesura in every line between the second and the third syllable. The three syllables following the caesura are not syntactically uniform which injects a lively element in to the 5-syllable *koshi*.

---

49. Yang Hsiung, styled Tzu-yün 子雲 (53 B.C.-18 A.D.), a native of Chengtu in Ssu-ch'uan, is a Confucian of Han dynasty who has left a work in 13 books, entitled *Fa Yen* 法言, and another work entitled *T'ai hsüan ching* 太玄經 (*Classic of the Great Mystery*). *Tai hsüan ching* is a work written in imitation of *I-ching* with the lines in groups of 4 rather than 6. Even at the time Yang Hsiung's contemporaries doubted the value of this abstruse work, and one of them commented that posterity would probably use it only as lids for sauce jars!!

50. *Ibid.*

51. *T'ung chih* 通志 is an historical encyclopaedia in 200 volumes, written by Cheng Ch'iao 鄭樵 (1104-1162) of the Sung dynasty covering institutions and literature from the earliest times down to the T'ang dynasty.

Translation 2

"Stirred By My Experience"

Form: *koshi*

Poem 3

					word no.	1	2	3	4	5
					line no.					
東	家	勢	炎	火						
高	樓	歌	管	起	2					@
北	鄰	貧	無	衣						
枵	腹	蓬	門	里	4					@
一	朝	高	樓	傾						
反	羨	北	鄰	子	6					@
盛	衰	各	遞	代						
難	可	逃	天	理	8					@

The mansion to the east is resplendent,
From its upper rooms, music resounds.[52]
Our northern neighbour is poor and threadbare:
Inside their humble house, empty bellies.
One morning the big mansion collapses
And rather envies the northern neighbour.
Success and failure come in turns;
It is hard to escape the decrees of fate.

Poem 4

					word no.	1	2	3	4	5
					line no.					
夜	夢	登	蓬	萊						
足	躡	葛	陂	龍	2					@
仙	人	綠	玉	杖						
邀	我	芙	蓉	峰	4					@
下	視	東	海	水						
澹	然	若	一	杯	6					@
花	下	鳳	吹	笙						
月	照	黃	金	罍	8					@

At night in dream I climbed Mt. Pongnae,
My feet on the dragon of Ko-p'o bank.

---

52. This (first 2 lines) is reminiscent of the 5th poem of the "Nineteen Old Poems" of the Han.

An immortal with a magic bamboo cane
Invited me to Lotus Hill.
I looked down on the Eastern Sea,
As tranquil as a cup of water.
Beneath the flowers a phoenix played the pan-pipes;
The moon shone on the golden jar.

Commentary

The title *Kan-yü* (Kor. *Kamu*) "Stirred by my Experience," was originally used by Ch'en Tzŭ-ang for his thirty eight poems, which is under the same category as Juan Chi's *Yung-huai* "Singing my Feeling." The predominant philosophical outlook in *kan-yü* is neo-Taoist—a theme of *hsien-jen shih-chih* (Kor. *hyŏnin shilchi*).

Nansŏrhŏn's four *kamu* poems are written in five-syllable *koshi*. These two *kamu* poems are the third and fourth of four included in her collection. The third poem clearly represents the inequalities of the material world, while the fourth is neo-Taoist in its expression of the ideal world for which she yearns. It appears that she has juxtapositioned two poems for evaluative purposes, setting the frailty of human existence against her own world of excellence—that of the immortal being. Here she envisages a flight beyond the bounds of the real world. The fourth *kamu* seems to be predominantly a philosophical piece—a rumination on social change which incorporates an element of social criticism.

Translation 3

"Mourning for My Children"

Form: *Koshi*

		word no.	1	2	3	4	5
		line no.					

去 年 喪 愛 女							
今 年 喪 愛 子	2						*
哀 哀 廣 陵 上							
雙 墳 相 對 起	4						*
蕭 蕭 白 楊 風							
鬼 火 明 松 楸	6						@
紙 錢 招 汝 魂							
玄 酒 奠 汝 丘	8						@
應 知 弟 兄 魂							
夜 夜 相 追 遊	10						@
縱 有 腹 中 孩							
安 可 冀 長 成	12						@
浪 吟 黃 臺 詞							
血 泣 悲 吞 聲	14						@

Last year I lost a dear daughter;
This year a dear son.
Sorrow, sorrow! In Kwangnŭng,[53]
Two graves[54] rise facing each other.
Gently, the white poplar whispers;
Ghost fires[55] light up pines and catalpas.
Paper money[56] welcomes your souls,
Holy water is offered at your tombs.
I should know how children's souls
Night after night, keep company together.

---

53. Kwangnŭng 廣陵, present Kwangju-gun, Kyŏnggi Province.
54. The graves of Nansŏrhŏn and her two children are on the hill in Kyŏngsu 鏡水, commonly called Kyŏngshi village, Ch'owŏl-li 草月里, Ch'owŏl-myŏn, Kwangju-gun, Kyŏnggi Province. The children's graves have been renovated in recent years. The creek in front of their graveyard is the lower part of Kyŏngan-ch'ŏn River 京安川 which is one of the tributaries of the Han River. The area is called Noŭn-so 老隱沼 derived from the pen name of Nansorhon's father-in-law Noŭn Kim. The site of the house is in Mora-kkol village where surviving roof tiles are still to be found.
55. "ghost fires" are will-o'-the-wisps (ignis fatuus).
56. Paper money refers to the square pieces of paper stamped with a dab of gold or silver and used in funeral observances. Burnt at Chinese Funerals, in Korea it was put into coffins.

Were one to have a babe in one's womb
How could one expect it to grow up?
Pointless to recite the "Yellow Terrace Lament,"[57]
With tears of blood, sorrow chokes my voice.

Commentary

Two rhymes are used in this poem, the first in deflected tone and the second in level tone. This change of rhyme brings some variation in the 5-syllable *koshi*. The lines are paired syntactically as couplets. Parallelism with antithesis and some repetition occurs between the lines of the first and fourth couplets: phonetic and semantic matching is brought about by the use of some identical words in corresponding positions. Reduplication of the characters which occurs at lines, 3, 5 and 10 is used for emphasis lending musical relief to the lament.

This poem was written in memory of her dead children. Hŏ Kyun writes that his sister never recovered from the tragic shock of losing both her children. Though he admits that after their death, she was able to devote most of her time to writing poetry, he was also certain that the loss of her children was the over-riding cause of her own untimely death. The blow undoubtedly fell more heavily upon Nansŏrhŏn because her relationship with her husband and in-laws was not entirely harmonious. The poem reveals the agonizing sorrow which she soothed by paying homage to her children's graves. She invoked their spirits by offering paper money and water as a token of their eventual reunion in the spirit world.

The imagery displayed—ghost fires in line 6, evoking dead spirits by burning paper money and offering holy water in lines 7 and 8, and the dead spirits of both brother and sister playing together in lines 9 and 10—is related to beliefs and practices that were widely accepted. This quality is echoed also in Li Ho's verse, (see Li Ho's poem on p. 36 above).

---

57. "Huang t'ai kua tz'u" 黃臺苽辭 was written by Li Hsien 李賢, the Crown Prince Chang-huai 章懷太子, sixth son of Emperor Kao-tsung 高宗 (r.649-83) of T'ang. It is included in *T'ang yin t'ung ch'ien* 唐音統籤 edited by Hu Chen-heng 胡震亨 (fl.1573-1602) of the Ming dynasty. See Hiraoka Takeo, *Tōdai no shijin*, Kyoto Daigaku. Jimbun Kagaku Kenkyūjo, 1960, p. 5. The poem describes the usurpation of Empress Wu 武后 (r.690-705), who, not content with ruling as Empress dowager, styled herself "Emperor" and changed the dynastic name from T'ang to Chou in 690, which shook the very foundation of the dynasty. See Liu, James J.Y., *The Poetry of Li Shang-yin*, (Chicago: The University of Chicago Press, 1969), p. 3.

Translation 4

"On Chasing Away Sad Thought"

Form: *Koshi*

Poem 5

					word no.	1	2	3	4	5
					line no.					
近	者	崔	白	輩						
攻	詩	軌	盛	唐	2					@
寥	寥	大	雅	音						
得	此	復	鏗	鏘	4					@
下	僚	困	光	祿						
邊	郡	愁	積	薪	6					@
年	位	共	零	落						
始	信	詩	窮	人	8					@

Recently the Ch'oe-Paek[58] poets
Write poetry in the High T'ang style.
With no echo of the Greater *Ya*,[59]
Now revived like a jingle of bells.
Lowly officials troubled by their superiors,
As problems were fueled in Border districts.
As their age and rank both decline,
They come to believe that poetry makes men poor.

Poem 8

					word no.	1	2	3	4	5
					line no.					
芳	樹	藹	初	綠						
麋	蕪	葉	已	齋	2					@
春	物	自	妍	華						
我	獨	多	悲	悷	4					@
壁	上	五	岳	圖						
床	頭	參	同	契	6					*
煉	丹	倘	有	成						
歸	謁	蒼	梧	帝	8					*

---

58. As stated earlier, Ch'oe and Paek were two of the Three T'ang Talents.
59. The Greater *Ya* is one of the four major divisions of the ancient Chinese poetic canon the *Shih ching*.

Fragrant trees flourish with fresh greenery;
Hemlock parsley already sprout everywhere.
In Spring, nature turns to elegant beauty;
But I alone am full of sadness and grief.
On my wall, a map of the Five Sacred Mountains;
At the table head is the *Ts'an t'ung ch'i*;
If my quest for the elixir succeeds,
I will pay homage to Emperor Shun.

Commentary

The titles *kyŏnhŭng* and *yung-huai* represent poetry of self-expression, being centred on the poet and his or her thought. *Yung-huai* which was first used by Juan Chi for his poetic masterpiece, a long series of eighty-two poems,[60] subsequently became the name of a poetic genre. Nansŏrhŏn's collection includes eight individual poems under the title *Kyŏnhŭng*. The two poems presented here are her fifth and eighth *kyŏnhŭng*.

Hŏ Kyun, in his *Haksan ch'odam,* verifies the fifth *kyŏnhŭng* as being written by the author in memory of Paek Kwanghun, one of the "Three T'ang Talents of Korea."[61] He cites the above *kyŏnhŭng* under the title of *Kamu*. There seems to be a discrepancy between the title Hŏ Kyun used in his *Haksan ch'odam* and that in Nansŏrhŏn's collection, although both titles represent poetry of the same category. The poem can also be regarded as evidence of how the group of poets who opposed the orthodox school suffered from lack of political and financial influence. It is one of a few source materials which reveal the poetic conventions within which Nansŏrhŏn wrote. The poem is also significant in that it gives some proof that Nansŏrhŏn might have tried to find immortality through Taoist alchemy and yoga. The last line alludes to a legend attributed to Emperor Shun and his two wives.[62]

---

60. See Donald Holzmann, *Poetry and Politics* (London: 1976), pp. 1-6.
61. See *HKCS*, p. 468.
62. See n. 65, p. 55 below.

Translation 5

"To Hagok"

Form: 5-syllable *koshi*

					word no.	1	2	3	4	5
					line no.					
暗	窗	銀	燭	低						
流	螢	度	高	閣	2					*
悄	悄	深	夜	寒						
蕭	蕭	秋	葉	落	4					*
關	河	音	信	稀						
端	憂	不	可	釋	6					*
遙	想	青	蓮	宮						
山	空	薜	月	白	8					*

By the dark window a silver candle burns low;
Fireflies flit across the high pavilion.
In the deep of night, I am anxious and cold;
Gently, autumn leaves fall.
News from the northern frontier is scarce;
I cannot restrain my endless worries.
From far away I think of Green Lotus Palace;[63]
On the empty mountain, shrubs breathe a bright moon.[64]

Commentary

This is one of the seven poems attributed to her brother Hŏ Pong, styled Hagok, who was sent in exile to Kapsan in 1583, to spend the following three years there. This poem is obviously written to him during his exile and makes use of the deflected tone, particularly the entering tone, to create the emotional atmosphere—moods of fearfulness, pathos and anxiety.

---

63. Ch'ŏngyŏn (Ch. Ch'ing lien) kung 靑蓮宮 is used in reference to the place where her brother, poet Hagok, resided during his exile. The fact that her brother was a brilliant poet himself seemed to have justified her use of Li Po's pen name, Ch'ing lien chu shih 靑蓮居士 (The Green Lotus Man), which Li Po is said to have borrowed from a Buddhist saint. See also Obata Shigeyoshi, trans., *The Works of Li Po* (Tokyo: 1935), p. 9.

64. Refer to Wang Wei's poem "Twenty Views of Wang-ch'uan: Deer Fence", Empty hills, no one in sight.

Translation 6

"Colouring Nails with Touch-me-not"

Form: 7-syllable *Koshi*

			word no.	1	2	3	4	5	6	7

line no.

Stanza 1

金 盆 夕 露 凝 紅 房　1　@
佳 人 十 指 纖 纖 長　2　@
竹 碾 搗 出 捲 菘 葉
燈 前 勤 護 雙 鳴 璫　4　@

Stanza 2

妝 樓 曉 起 廉 初 捲　5　*
喜 看 火 星 拋 鏡 面　6　*
拾 草 疑 飛 紅 蛺 蝶
彈 箏 驚 落 桃 花 片　8　*

Stanza 3

徐 勻 粉 頰 整 羅 鬢　9　@
湘 竹 臨 江 淚 血 斑　10　@
時 把 彩 毫 描 卻 月
只 疑 紅 雨 過 春 山　12　@

Evening dew in the golden saucer turns icy in the woman's quarters;
Ten fingers of a beautiful woman: slender and delicate.
The balsam is pounded in a bamboo mortar, then wrapped in cabbage
   leaves;
In the lamplight I wrapped it round my finger nails; my twin earrings
   chime.
Waking in the morning and lifting up the blinds of my dressing room,
I am delighted to see bright reflections in the mirror.
If I pluck grass it seems like a red-spotted butterfly in flight;
Playing the lute, I am surprised to see falling petals of peach blossoms.
When I gently powder my cheeks or tidy my silky hair,
I see tears of blood on speckled bamboos by River Hsiang:[65]
Brushing in my curved eyebrows, they seem like
Scarlet raindrops sweeping over the Spring mountains.

---

65. 湘江 a large tributary of the Yangtze which flows through Hunan; 湘(妃)竹: a speckled bamboo which grows in Hunan and Kwangsi. Legend has it that the bamboo became speckled by the tears which the wives of Emperor Shun 舜 (legendary emperor who succeeded Emperor Yao) shed over his grave.

Commentary

The *koshi* is divided into three stanzas by the use of a separate rhyme for each stanza. The rhyming words are always at the end of the first line of the stanza, and at the end of each even numbered line. The first and the last stanzas have the rhyme occurring in level tone and the middle stanza in deflected tone, which is not uncommon with *koshi*. There is a major caesura between fourth and fifth syllables and a minor one between second and third which makes the syntax structure uniform throughout the poem. The change of rhyme may be to break the monotony of syntactically paired couplets. Each stanza consists of four lines of a uniform length of seven syllables. All three stanzas are linked to both the preceding and the following stanza by topical linkage.

The poem neither lends itself easily to translation nor humours those who are alien to the out-moded female custom of colouring nails with balsam on a cool Korean autumn evening. The girls took great care to gather only the best balsam blossoms, pound them to ensure good results, wrap them around their fingers and leave them overnight to colour the nails. After an anxious night of little sleep they might wake to the surprise of having beautifully-coloured red nails, a result which added excitement to their search for inner beauty.

Translation 7

"Song of the Magic Strings by the River Hsiang"

Form: 7-syllable *koshi*

	word no.	1	2	3	4	5	6	7
	line no.							
	Stanza 1							
蕉 花 泣 露 湘 江 曲	1							*
九 點 秋 煙 天 外 綠	2							*
水 府 涼 波 龍 夜 吟								
蠻 娘 輕 憂 玲 瓏 玉	4							*
	Stanza 2							
離 鸞 別 鳳 隔 蒼 梧	5							@
雨 氣 侵 江 迷 曉 珠	6							@
閑 撥 神 絃 石 璧 上								
花 鬟 月 鬢 啼 江 姝	8							@
	Stanza 3							
瑤 空 星 漢 高 超 忽	9							*
羽 蓋 金 支 五 雲 沒	10							*
門 外 漁 郎 唱 竹 枝								
銀 潭 半 掛 相 思 月	12							*

Banana flowers weep dew at the bend of the River Hsiang;
Over the nine peaks an autumn mist, the sky fringed with green.
In the underwater palace the waves are chill and dragons
    roar at night;
A Southern girl touched by grief is like elegant jade.
The male phoenix has flown away to distant Mt. Ts'ang-wu;
The rain-filled air shrouds the river, dimming the dawn light.
At leisure, high on the cliff, she plucks the magic strings;
With tresses of flowers and moonlight the Hsiang beauties weep.
In a sky of Jade, the distant ramparts of the Milky Way.
Parasols with golden shafts drown in multi-coloured clouds.
Outside the gate fishermen sing the Bamboo Branch song;
Over a silvery lake the moon of longing lovers droops halfway.

Commentary

This poem is heavily influenced by the "Chiu ko" (Nine Songs) of *Ch'u-tz'u*, particularly the third song, "Hsiang chün" (Kor. Sang gun) [The Princess of the Hsiang] and the fourth song, "Hsiang fu jen" (Kor. Sang puin) ["The Lady of the Hsiang"]. Both songs describe a female or male shaman's performance, drawing the gods down from heaven in a kind of courtship.

Translation 8

"Poems for the Four Seasons"

Form: 7-syllable *koshi*

Spring

word no.	1	2	3	4	5	6	7
line no.							

Stanza 1

院	落	深	沈	杏	花	雨	1		*
流	鶯	啼	在	辛	夷	塢	2		*
流	蘇	羅	幕	襲	春	寒			
博	山	輕	飄	香	一	縷	4		*

Stanza 2

美	人	睡	罷	理	新	妝	5		@
香	羅	寶	帶	蟠	鴛	鴦	6		@
斜	捲	重	簾	帖	翡	翠			
懶	把	銀	箏	彈	鳳	凰	8		@

Stanza 3

金	勒	雕	鞍	去	何	處	9		*
多	情	鸚	鵡	當	窗	語	10		*
草	粘	戲	蝶	庭	畔	迷			
花	胃	游	絲	闌	外	舞	12		*

Stanza 4

誰	家	池	館	咽	笙	歌	13		@
月	照	美	酒	金	叵	羅	14		@
愁	人	獨	夜	不	成	寐			
曉	起	鮫	綃	紅	淚	多	16		@

In the courtyard, a shower of peach petals piles deep;
Wandering orioles cry out on a magnolia tree near the fence.
Through tasseled silk curtains the spring cold seeps in;
From the censer[66] a wisp of burning incense gently curls.
A beautiful girl woken from sleep makes up her face anew;
Fine girdle of fragrant silk; patterned with ducks.
She rolls up a thick blind, revealing the kingfisher curtain;
Unhurried, she plays the phoenix song on her silver zither.
Where has her Lord gone on his gold-engraved saddle?

---

66. Po-shan lu (Kor. Paksan no) 博山爐: the name of the censer. Po Shan is said to be one of many mountains where immortals dwell. See Lü Ta-lin 呂大臨 (d. ca. 1090), *K'ao ku t'u* 考古圖, 1297-1307? ed.

A friendly parrot chatters at the window; a butterfly
Sports in the grasses, then flits along the garden path,
Dancing among the flowers, gossamers outside the door.
Sounds of flutes and song from a neighbours house;
The moon shines on a golden cup of fine wine.
At night, she is quite alone and unable to sleep;
At dawn she wakes, tears soaking the shagreen silk.

Summer

	word no.	1	2	3	4	5	6	7
	line no.							
Stanza 1								
槐 陰 滿 地 花 陰 薄	1							*
玉 簟 銀 床 敞 珠 閣	2							*
白 苧 衣 裳 汗 凝 珠								
呼 風 羅 扇 搖 羅 幕	4							*
Stanza 2								
瑤 階 開 盡 石 榴 花	5							@
日 轉 華 簷 簾 影 斜	6							@
雕 梁 晝 永 燕 引 雛								
藥 欄 無 人 蜂 報 衙	8							@
Stanza 3								
刺 繡 倦 來 午 眠 重	9							@
錦 茵 敲 落 釵 頭 鳳	10							@
額 上 鵝 黃 膩 睡 痕								
流 鶯 喚 起 江 南 夢	12							@
Stanza 4								
南 塘 女 伴 木 蘭 舟	13							@
采 采 荷 花 歸 渡 頭	14							@
輕 橈 齊 唱 采 菱 曲								
驚 起 波 間 雙 白 鷗	16							@

A *Sophora* tree[67] shades the ground and outlines of the flowers;
Jade mat and silver bed seem spacious in a pearl mansion.
Sweat forms like beads in the white hemp robe;
A fan of silk gauze stirs the wind, rustling the silk curtain.
By the jade steps the pomegranate is in full bloom;
The sun brightens the ornate eaves, and blinds cast oblique shadows.

---

67. A large tree which grows in North China; it is a kind of loquat, the flowers are used for yellow dye, the timber is useful. *Sophora japonica.*

A swallow in the carved beams all day long, leads her nestlings out;
No one at the garden fence; the bees sound busy.
She tires of embroidering and dozes in the hot afternoon;
Her phoenix hairpin drops, falling on a silk cushion.
On her forehead, thin yellow grease; the remains of sleep.
A cuckoo on the wing wakes her from some romantic dream.
Friends from the southern pond, in a magnolia boat,
Have gathered the lotus flowers and return to the quay.[68]
They row gently singing the water-chestnut song.
They startle and rouse a pair of white gulls on the water.

Commentary

Sashi sa consists of four poems, each representing a season of the year. It is generally accepted that poems of this ilk correspond to the four movements of a musical composition. Each poem is normally linked to the next, and the thematic material is transferred from one seasonal mood to another. In spite of contrasts between the moods, the poems have a sense of unity. For this reason the four poems should be treated as parts of a whole. To give equal treatment to various forms, as well as to the themes of Nansŏrhŏn's poems, only two out of four of her rather lengthy *Sashi sa* (sixteen lines of seven syllables each) are presented here. These poems are basically love songs, set on a variation in mood, influenced by the changing seasons.

The peach blossom and magnolia tree in the first couplet of the first poem represent early Spring, in which a girl longs for her lover. Nansŏrhŏn paints Spring as the provocative season, although she casts it in a melancholic atmosphere. The falling peach blossoms and crying orioles in lines 1-2 and the Spring chill, with a shred of burning incense in 3-4, set the somewhat sorrowful mood in which the girl pines for her lover, and becomes dispirited. Her need for love is expressed symbolically—mandarin ducks in line 6, a kingfisher in line 7 and a phoenix in line 8.

The curtain and the blind in the fourth couplet are used as a barrier to isolate the boudoir from the outside world, thus focusing on the contrast between the two worlds. This technique is frequently used in Chinese and Sino-Korean poetry to highlight the theme by either discords or correspondences. The lovelorn girl inside contrasts with the amorous parrot which symbolizes the united couple, thus emphasizing her loneliness. Lines 11 and 12 also indicate a sad mood in which the girl's longing corresponds to the darting butterfly.

---

68. See Wang Wei's poem entitled, 山中即事.

In the second poem the first two couplets set the scene on a Summer's afternoon. The white hemp costume and silk fan endorse the summer heat. Overcome by the hot day and the unending frustration of waiting in vain, the girl falls asleep. She still has not given up hope and dreams of the romantic land south of the River Yangtze but is abruptly brought back to reality by the plaintive cry of a love-sick cuckoo.

Translation 9

"Song of Free From Care" [69]

Form: see commentary

Poem 1

word no.	1	2	3	4	5
line no.					

		line no.		2		4	5
家 住 石 城 下	1		X		O	
生 長 石 城 頭	2		O		O	@
嫁 得 石 城 婿	3		X		O	
來 往 石 城 游	4		X		O	@

My house is at Shih-ch'eng;[70]
I was brought up in Shih-ch'eng;
I married a man from Shih-ch'eng;
I visit Shih-ch'eng to play.

Poem 2

word no.	1	2	3	4	5
line no.					

		line no.		2		4	5
儂 住 白 玉 堂	1		X		X	
郎 騎 五 花 馬	2		O		O	*
朝 日 石 城 頭	3		X		O	
春 江 戲 雙 舸	4		O		O	*

Earlier I lived in the White Jade Hall;[71]
My husband used to ride the dappled horse.[72]
When the sun rose over Shih-ch'eng,
We sported in twin boats on the spring river.

Commentary

YFSC includes four songs on Mo-ch'ou, three entitled *Mo-ch'ou yüeh* (Kor. *Maksu ak*) and one *Mo-ch'ou ch'ü* (Kor. *Maksu kok*) under *Ch'ing-shang ch'ü-tz'u,* chapter 48. The commentary explains that these songs are about a

---

69. Mo-ch'ou 莫愁, literally, "Never sorrow" or "Don't Worry," is the name of a singing girl who lived in Shih-ch'eng, "Rocky City." See commentary.

70. Shih-ch'eng 石城: Chung-hsiang County, Hupeh.

71. Government official's residence.

72. The spotted horse. See Li Po's Poem entitled "An Exhortation" (將進酒), Obata Shigeyoshi, *op. cit.,* pp. 86-87.

singing girl from Shih-ch'eng who was called Mo-ch'ou (meaning "never sorrow" or "Sans Souci") and her lover. The poem is originally from *Shih-ch'eng yüeh* (Kor. *Sŏksŏng ak*) of *Ch'ing-shan ch'ü-tz'u,* chapter 47. Likewise, Nansŏrhŏn's *maksu-ak* belongs to the *Hsi-ch'u ko* (Kor. *Sŏgok ka*) of *Ch'ing- shang ch'ü-tz'u,* chapter 48, which as noted above can be traced back to the love songs of the Southern Dynasties. During the Southern Dynasties the *yüeh-fu* songs of the Han became more standarized in form and became more lyrical than narrative in nature. Hans H. Frankel points out that the prevailing pattern in both Southern and Northern Dynasties is four lines of five syllables each—a forerunner of the *chüeh-chu* of the T'ang dynasty.[73] During the T'ang dynasty it was not uncommon to cast *yüeh-fu* ballads in *chüeh-chu* or even in regulated verse.[74]

Nansŏrhŏn's *Maksu ak* is written in the pattern of four lines of five syllables. Poem One has rhyme in level tone at the end of each couplet. It does not observe any fixed tonal patterns and has repetition of identical words in corresponding positions in each line. This phenomenon of complete phonetic and semantic matching in neighbouring lines is rather rare and occurs in those poetic genres which originated from songs such as *Shih ching, yüeh-fu* and *tz'u.* As mentioned earlier, in Chinese and Sino-Korean poetry the prevailing tendency is to keep phonetic dissimilarity between corresponding syllables in the two lines of a couplet. The diction is quite plain and straightforward. The whole atmosphere of this poem suggests an *akpu* song or a forerunner of *chŏlgu* which is more common in the Six Dynasties' *yeüeh-fu* song than in *chüeh-chu* of the T'ang period. Her *maksu ak* is very similar to the following *Mo-ch'ou yüeh* by Chang Hu (fl. first half of 9th century) of the T'ang period:

儂 居 石 城 下
郎 到 石 城 遊
自 郎 石 城 出
自 在 石 城 頭

　　　—See *YFSC*, Matching Songs, chapter 48.

Poem Two has rhyme in deflected tone at the end of each couplet and does not observe any fixed tonal patterns. The deflected tone in rhyme words enhances the melancholy tone in which the heroine reflects on happier days.

---

73. Hans H. Frankel, *Yüeh-fu Poetry, op. cit.,* p. 95.
74. See pp. 33 above.

Translation 10

"Song for the Poor Girl"

Form: 5-character *chŏlgu*

Poem 1

	word no.	1	2	3	4	5
	line no.					
豈 是 乏 容 色	1		X		O	*
工 鍼 復 工 織	2		O		O	*
少 小 長 寒 門	3		X		O	
良 媒 不 相 識	4		O		O	*

> Surely she does not lack beauty
> Nor skills in sewing and weaving.
> But she grew up in a poor family
> So good matchmakers ignore her.

Poem 2

	word no.	1	2	3	4	5
	line no.					
不 帶 寒 餓 色	1		X		X	*
盡 日 當 窗 織	2		X		O	*
唯 有 父 母 憐	3		X		X	
四 鄰 何 會 識	4		O		O	*

> She never looks cold or hungry,
> All day long she weaves by the window.
> Only her parents feel sorry for her;
> Neighbours would never know of it.

Poem 3

	word no.	1	2	3	4	5
	line no.					
夜 久 織 未 休	1		X		X	@
戛 戛 鳴 寒 機	2		X		O	@
機 中 一 疋 練	3		O		X	
終 作 阿 誰 衣	4		X		O	@

> Into the long night she weaves without rest,
> Creak, creak, goes the cold loom.
> The roll of dressed silk in the frame;
> Whose clothes is she weaving after all?

Poem 4

	word no.	1	2	3	4	5
	line no.					
手 把 金 剪 刀	1		X		X	
夜 寒 十 指 直	2		O		X	*
為 人 作 嫁 衣	3		O		X	
年 年 還 獨 宿	4		O		X	*

A pair of golden scissors in her hand,
Fingers stiffened by the night's chill.
She cuts a bridal costume for another,
Yet year after year she sleeps alone.

Commentary

Two problem points should be recognized with these poems. Firstly, they are treated in Nansŏrhŏn's collection as four individual verses under one title, which is not uncommon with *hanshi*. It would, however, be appropriate to catalogue them as one poem with four stanzas, because of the continuity of description. Secondly, the third stanza, which O Haein includes in her edition of *Nansŏrhŏn chip*, differs from the other stanzas. O Haein points out that the third stanza is included in *Li tai nu tzu shih chi* as the work of the wife of the T'ang poet, Yü Ju-chou.[75] I have been unable to locate this collection, and cannot therefore confirm this. Notwithstanding this, an analysis of the form has led me to believe there is a strong possibility that this poem is not Nansŏrhŏn's. The reason for this belief is that the 1st, 2nd and 4th stanzas observe the *chŏlgu* rule, in which there are single rhymes in deflected tone at the end of the 1st, 2nd and 4th line of each stanza, whereas the 3rd stanza alone has level tone for its rhyme. It is common to have rhyme in level tone in *chŏlgu*, but rhyme does not change in the course of the poem. None of the four stanzas follow a fixed tonal pattern.

Nansŏrhŏn was born and bred in a *yangban* family. Unlike the majority of women who had the same family background however, she showed a remarkable understanding and sympathy for the deprived groups of society—women of poor families, *kisaeng*, palace ladies, etc. Her father, although he held high office in government, was content to be poor, and he remained incorruptible. This is one of several of her poems which are written allegorically as an expression of protest against social injustice. As her poem relates: a beautiful girl with many talents, must needs earn money by slavishly labouring day and night to weave the bridal garments of others; all the while knowing she holds no attraction for the matchmakers.

---

75. *NSC*, p. 118.

Translation 11

"Imitation of Ts'ui Kuo-fu's[76] Style"

Form: *akpu*

Poem 1

中文	word no.	1	2	3	4	5
	line no.					
妾 有 黃 金 釵	1		X		O	
嫁 時 為 首 飾	2		O		X	*
今 日 贈 君 行	3		X		O	
千 里 長 相 憶	4		X		O	*

I have a golden hairpin,

An ornament from my wedding.

Today it is a present for your journey;

Think of me when a thousand miles away.

Poem 2

中文	word no.	1	2	3	4	5
	line no.					
池 頭 楊 柳 疏	1		O		X	
井 上 梧 桐 落	2		X		O	*
簾 外 候 蟲 聲	3		X		O	
天 寒 錦 衾 薄	4		O		O	*

Over the pond a willow, thinning;

On the well, paulownia leaves fall.

Outside the window blind, insects chirp.

Chill of autumn. A thin embroidered quilt.

Poem 3

中文	word no.	1	2	3	4	5
	line no.					
春 雨 暗 西 池	1		X		O	
輕 寒 襲 羅 幕	2		O		O	*
愁 倚 小 屏 風	3		X		O	
牆 頭 杏 花 落	4		O		O	*

Spring rain dims the west pool;

A slight chill penetrates the silk blind.

Feeling sad, my elbow on the bed screen;

Beyond the fence plum blossoms fall.

---

76. Ts'ui Kuo-fu 崔國輔 (687-755).

Commentary

This poem is one of her three imitations of the literary works of the T'ang poets. T'sui Kuo-fu's *yüeh-fu, Yüan-shih* "The Forsaken Wife" in two stanzas of five-syllable lines was the model she used. In her pattern and wording she follows his poem quite closely in the second and third stanza, except that she adds, at the beginning, the introductory stanza of giving her departing husband a keepsake. This makes the poem more personal. Both poems have single rhyme in deflected tone at the end of each couplet, which sets the general sad tone. In tonal pattern she closely imitates her model:

Nansŏrhŏn's tonal pattern	*Ts'ui Kuo-fu's tonal pattern*
1st stanza	
X O	
O X X	
X O	
X O X	
2nd stanza	*1st stanza*
O X	O X
X O X	X O X
X O	X X
O O X	O O X
3rd stanza	*2nd stanza*
X O	X O
O O X	O O X
X O	X O
O O X	O O X

Though it is treated in her collection as an ordinary *shi* of five-syllable *chŏlgu* "quatrain," the fact that the poem does not follow the fixed tonal pattern (though not unusual in a quatrain) and its theme of women neglected by their menfolk, being drawn from the *akpu* tradition (*YFSC*, ch. 42, Matching Songs), places it in the category of *akpu*. There is contrast between the outside world with its trees and flowers shedding their blossom and the inside world of a single womanly figure, a silk coverlet and a small screen.

Translation 12

"Song of Ch'ang-kan"[77]

Form: see commentary

Poem 1

					word no.	1	2	3	4	5
					line no.					
家	居	長	干	里	1		O		O	
來	往	長	干	道	2		X		O	@
折	花	問	阿	郎	3		O		O	
何	如	妾	貌	好	4		O		X	@

My home was in Ch'ang-kan[78] town;
I used to walk along its streets.
There I plucked flowers and asked you.
"Was I as beautiful?"

Poem 2

					word no.	1	2	3	4	5
					line no.					
昨	夜	南	風	興	1		X		O	
船	旗	指	巴	水	2		O		O	@
逢	著	北	來	人	3		X		O	
知	君	在	揚	州	4		O		O	@

Last night a south wind blew;
The boat's flag pointed to Yangtze.[79]
I met someone coming from the North,
But I know that you were in Yang-chou.[80]

Commentary

Nansŏrhŏn's *Changgan-haeng* is cast in four lines of five syllables each and is classified as a five-syllable *chŏlgu* in her collection. Notwithstanding this, there are four points which portray it as belonging to the *akpu* song.

---

77. Refer to Li Po's 李伯 "Two Letters from Ch'ang-kan" 長干行, 一, 二, Obata Shigeyoshi, *Li Po: The Chinese Poet* (New York:1928), pp. 151-154. Ezra Pound has also done a version of the first poem.
78. Ch'ang-kan 長干 is a village which is located south of the River Ch'in-huai, now a suburb of Nanking. It used to be a quay.
79. Pa-shui (Kor. P'asu): is presently by River Pa in Hupei: upper Yangtze region.
80. Yang-chou is a prefecture in Kiangsu.

First, the rhyme changes in the course of the poem; the first stanza has a rhyme at the end of each couplet in level tone, whereas the second is in two conflicting tones. The rhyme words of the second stanza *su* at the end of the first couplet is in deflected tone and *chu* at the end of the second couplet, is in level tone. Of course, this could be no more than a simple mistake. Second, the poem does not observe the fixed tonal pattern. Third, there is repetition of the word Ch'ang-kan in the same metric position, creating a musical effect. Fourth, *Changgan haeng*[81] is a traditional *akpu* title which can be traced back, at least to the Southern Dynasties.

Ch'ang-kan hsing is a love song which portrays the forlorn love of a merchant's wife pining for her husband, who is a trader and away from home. Ch'ang-kan is well known for its beautiful scenery along the river bank, and Li Po is said to have been very fond of the village.

The juxtaposition of a happy past in poem one and the lonely present combined with separation in the second poem sharpen the pain of loneliness felt by a wife who stays behind. Companionship is coupled with separation and happiness with grief to highlight the emptiness of separation. The sense of seperation is also achieved by the juxtaposition of two pairs of place names between two stanzas. In the second poem Nansŏrhŏn employs a few standard images associated with the parting, such as river, wind and boat. The wind is regarded as a favourite image of separation, as its unpredictable movement creates a mood of instability and discomfort, indicative of separation. The boat symbolizes travel across the water, which in turn creates an impassable barrier separating the couple.

---

81. *YFSC* includes nine poems on Ch'ang-kan village, variously titled as *Ch'ang-kan hsing* (Kor. *Changgan haeng*), *Ch'ang-kan chü* (Kor. *Changgan kok*), and *Hsiao Ch'ang-kan ch'ü* (Kor. *So Changgan kok*) are under Miscellaneous Songs, Chapter 72. Of the nine, one is *Ku-tz'ü* (Kor. *kosa*, Anonymous Old Folksong) bearing this title; two are by Li Po and four by Ts'ui Hao (704-754) of T'ang.

Translation 13

"Song of the Land South of the River"

Form: see commentary

Poem 1

	word no.	1	2	3	4	5
	line no.					
江 南 風 日 好	1		O		X	
綺 羅 金 翠 翹	2		O		X	@
相 將 採 菱 去	3		O		O	
齊 盪 木 蘭 橈	4		O		O	@

The Land South of the River[82] is a good place:
Open silk dresses and gold feathered caps.
Together people go to collect water-chestnuts;
In unison, they ply their magnolia oars.[83]

Poem 2

	word no.	1	2	3	4	5
	line no.					
人 言 江 南 樂	1		O		O	
我 見 江 南 愁	2		X		O	@
年 年 沙 浦 口	3		O		X	
腸 斷 望 歸 舟	4		X		O	@

People say South of the River is enjoyable
But to me sorrow abides there.
Every year at the port's sand bar
My heart breaks to see the returning boat.

Poem 3

	word no.	1	2	3	4	5
	line no.					
湖 里 月 初 明	1		X		O	
采 蓮 中 夜 歸	2		O		X	@
輕 橈 莫 近 岸	3		O		X	
恐 驚 鴛 鴦 飛	4		O		O	@

---

82. South of the River Yangtze, the provinces of Kiangsu and Anhwei.
83. Near the River Kiukang in the Land South of the River, there used to be many dead magnolia trees which were used to make boats and oars.

Reflected by the lake,[84] a new moon shines;
Lotus gatherers go home at midnight.
Little boat, don't go near the shore!
A pair of mandarin ducks[85] may be scared away.

Poem 4

					word no. line no.	1	2	3	4	5
生	長	江	南	村	1	O		O		
少	年	無	別	離	2	O		X		@
那	知	年	十	五	3	O		X		
嫁	與	弄	潮	兒	4	X		O		@

Born and raised in a South River village[86]
A young girl has never been parted.
How could she know, at fifteen,[87]
That she would marry a boatman.

Poem 5

					word no. line no.	1	2	3	4	5
紅	藕	作	裙	衩	1		X		O	
白	蘋	為	雜	佩	2		O		X	*
停	舟	下	渚	邊	3		O		X	
共	待	寒	潮	退	4		X		O	*

Pink lotusroot woven into skirts and jackets;
With white waterweed[88] for floral posies.
Mooring the boat, they alight on the island's shore,
And wait together for the cold tide to ebb.

Commentary

In Nansŏrhŏn's collection, these poems are catalogued as five-syllable *chŏlgu*. There are however a number of features which indicate that they rather belong to *akpu* songs. These are:

---

84. The Lake T'ai-hu in Chiang-nan.
85. The mandarin duck, male and female, used as an emblem of conjugal fidelity and happiness.
86. South of the River Yangtze.
87. This also refers to Li Po's 長干行.
88. Paekpin 白蘋 is translated as "whiteweed" by J.A. Turner in his translation of Weng T'ing-yun's poem entitled 憶江南 (To the Tune of Dreaming of South River Land), *The Golden Treasury of Chinese Poetry*, (Hong Kong:1976), p. 193 and as "white artemesia" by Ann Birrel, *op. cit.*, p. 146.

1. *Kangnam kok* (Ch. *Chiangnan-ch'ü*)[89] is a traditional *akpu* title, dating back at least to the Liang dynasty.

2. There are repetitions of words within poem and monosyllables within line which lend themselves to the musical effect of songs, rather than *chŏlgu shi*. An example is the use of the identical word *Kangnam* in corresponding position of the first couplet in stanza two and the reduplication of *nyŏn nyŏn* 年年 in line three of the second stanza.

3. The rhyme changes in the course of the poem from level tone to deflected tone. This change of rhyme is more common in *koshi* form than *kŭnch'e shi*.

In the first poem, Nansŏrhŏn sets an idyllic scene: the exquisite charm of the southern countryside in line 1; luxurious and sensuous garments worn by the beautiful girls of the Yangtze region in line 2; the chestnut gathering— traditionally linked with the romantic love songs of South China in line 3 and finally rowing the boat with oars made of magnolia wood which is said to be abundant in the region, in line 4. This presentation of beautiful scenery effectively sharpens the pain of loneliness which follows in poem two. The second poem starts with a parallel couplet which alludes to the loneliness of the boatman's wife. It employs such words as, river, bank and boat, all of which are words traditionally used to imply either parting or separation. There is a parallelism in three levels in the first couplet:

1. Grammatical parallelism occurs by matching subject *in* 人 (people), and *a* 我 (I); verbs *ŏn* 言 (to say) and *kyŏn* 見 (to see); objects of compound words *Kangnam ak* 江南樂 (...that Kangnam is pleasant) and *Kangnam su* 江南愁 (...that Kangnam is sorrowful).

2. These grammatically-matching words belong to the same category but differ in meaning, thereby creating a semantic parallelism.

3. The repetition of identical words such as *Kangnam* in the corresponding positions not only invites coordination but is also musically effective.

These phenomena of parallelism give an aesthetically pleasing effect to the couplet. Poem three sets the romantic evening scene at South of the River, with the conventional description of a woman who is longing for her lover or

---

89. The theme of *Kangnam kok* is said to have originated from the Han folksong called *Chiangnan*, which portrays life in the fishing villages South of the Yangtze River. During the Wei dynasty this song was, for the first time, included in the Matching Songs. *YFSC* includes twenty-seven poems of *Chiangnan ch'ü* under *Hsiang-ho ko tz'u* "Matching Songs" in chapter 26. Of the twenty-seven the two earliest songs are written one each by Liu Yun (465-511) and Shen Yueh (441-512) of the Liang dynasty. The other twenty-five poems are the compositions of various T'ang poets such as Li Shang-yin, Li Ho, Wen T'ing-yun (812-870) et. al.

husband. The lotus gatherers, in line 3, imply the love song of the Southern Dynasties: the mandarin ducks, in line 4 are associated with the happy couple which generates the mood of the yearning for love. These poems, in general, portray the woman as a victim of unrequited love, submissively accepting her fate.

Translation 14

"Song of a Walk in Skyland"[90]

Form: see commentary

Poem 1

							word no.	1	2	3	4	5	6	7
							line no.							
乘	鸞	夜	下	蓬	萊	島	1		O		X		O	*
閒	輾	麟	車	踏	瑤	草	2		X		O		O	*
海	風	吹	折	碧	桃	花	3		O		X		O	
玉	盤	滿	摘	安	期	棗	4		O		X		O	*

By night she rides a phoenix to the Blessed Isles,[91]
On a chariot drawn by unicorns over jade grass.
A sea breeze blows, scattering the jade peach blossoms;[92]
The jade tray is filled with the dates of An-ch'i.[93]

Commentary

Hŏ Kyun in his *Haksan ch'odam* points out that his sister, Nansŏrhŏn, wrote the *Pohŏ sa* (Ch. *Pu-hsu tz'u*) in imitation of that of Liu Yu-hsi (772-842). *YFSC* includes forty-eight poems of *Pu-hsu tz'u* under *Ts'a-ch'ü ko tz'ü* (Kor. *Chapkok kasa*) "Miscellaneous Songs," Chapter 78. Of these, two are written by Liu Yu-hsi, the earliest being the two poems by Emperor Yang of Sui dynasty. *Pu-shu tz'u* is a Taoist song which describes the beauty of the misty and superlunary country of the immortals. (see *YFSC* chapter 78).

Her model (two *pu-hsu tz'u*) is cast in four lines of seven syllables each. The poem has rhymes at the end of the first, second and the third lines in deflected tone and Nansŏrhŏn follows the same pattern. Neither she nor Liu Yu-hsi observe any fixed tonal pattern as the following chart illustrates:

---

90. *Hsü* (Kor. *Hŏ*) 虛: the god of the constellation, See DCM, p. 173.
91. See n. 24, p. 35 above.
92. The peaches said to grow in the K'un-lun Mountain and to be served at P'an- t'ao Hui, the periodical banquet of the Immortals.
93. An-ch'i (An-ch'i Sheng) 安期生: a magician from the Shantung coast favoured by the first Ch'in Emperor. He disappeared, leaving a letter in which he invited the emperor to meet him in two years' time on the fairy island of P'eng-lai. The imposter Li Hsiao-chun 李小君 boasted to Emperor Wu of the Han dynasty that he had been to sea and saw An-ch'i Sheng eating dates as big as melons. See David Hawkes, *op. cit.*, p. 179.

Nansŏrhŏn	*Liu Yu-hsi*
O X O *	X O X *
X O O *	X O O *
O X O	O X O
O X O *	X O O *

The form and theme of this poem indicates that it is written as *akpu* or forerunner of *chŏlgu*.

Translation 15

"Courtesan's Song"

Form: 7-syllable *chŏlgu*

						word no.	1	2	3	4	5	6	7
						line no.							
夾	道	青	樓	十	萬	家	1		X		O		X	@
家	家	門	巷	七	香	車	2		O		X		O	@
東	風	吹	折	相	思	柳	3		O		X		O	
細	馬	驕	行	踏	落	花	4		X		O		X	@

Lining the narrow street, lots of brothels;
At every gate sumptuous carriages.[94]
An east wind blows and snaps the willow branch of love;
Riding a fine horse, a man gallops over fallen flowers.

Commentary

Unlike the conventional courtesan's song, in which a beautiful woman in one of
the more refined brothels is longing for her special lover, and thereby enhancing
the erotic element, this poem has the antithesis of the privileged man and the
deprived prostitute. The description progresses from the narrow street where the
many brothels are located, to the numerous richly-adorned carriages, producing a
vivid contrast between lower and upper classes. Nansŏrhŏn is implying that this
is the lustful act of a high-ranking man, who exploits a disadvantaged woman,
riding roughshod over her love for him. However, rather than being merely an
erotic poem, it conveys more of a social protest.

---

94. This may refer to sandalwood: see sandalwood carriage (沈香輦), Liu Ts'un-yen, *op. cit.*,
p. 136

Translation 16

"Swing Song"

Form: 7-syllable *chŏlgu*

							word no.	1	2	3	4	5	6	7
							line no.							
鄰	家	女	伴	競	鞦	韆	1		O		X		O	@
結	帶	蟠	巾	學	半	仙	2		X		O		X	@
風	送	綵	繩	天	上	去	3		X		O		X	
佩	聲	時	落	綠	楊	煙	4		O		X		O	@

Neighbour women compete on the swings; belts tied
And kerchiefs round their heads, resemble Immortals.
The coloured ropes soar up to the sky.
Bangles clunk amid hazy green willows.

							word no.	1	2	3	4	5	6	7
							line no.							
蹴	罷	鞦	韆	整	繡	鞋	1		X		O		X	@
下	來	無	語	立	瑤	階	2		O		X		O	@
蟬	衫	細	濕	輕	輕	汗	3		O		X		O	
忘	卻	教	人	拾	墜	釵	4		X		O		X	@

Swinging finished, she straightens her embroidered shoes,
Descends and stands silent on emerald steps:
Gauze jacket lightly beaded with sweat, she forgets
To order anyone to retrieve her fallen haircomb.

Commentary

O Haein points out that the second stanza is also included in *Li tai nu tz'u shih chi* as a work of Lady Ch'eng.[95] The poem describes one of the festival activities which is taking place in the festival called *tanojŏl*. The day is one of a few when Chosŏn dynasty women were legally allowed to go out of their houses to join in public functions. The longing for the immortal land is displayed by employing the analogy between the ornamentation of the mortal world and the world of the immortals. The juxtaposition is built on the correspondences between two worlds: the two girls dressed ready for the swing symbolize the figurines of immortals in line 2 of the first stanza and the "wind blowing the colourful rope up to the sky" in line 3 of the same stanza is the image of immortals ascending to the Blessed Land.

---

95. I am unable to support her statement, as it was not possible for me to obtain this collection.

Translation 17

"Palace Song"

Form: 7-syllable *Chŏlgu*

Poem 1

word no.	1	2	3	4	5	6	7
line no.							
千 牛 閣 下 放 朝 初 1		O		X		O	@
擁 帚 宮 人 掃 玉 除 2		X		O		X	@
日 午 殿 頭 宣 詔 語 3		X		O		X	
隔 簾 催 喚 女 尚 書 4		O		X		O	@

Ch'ŏnu Pavilion fronts the early morning;
Maids with brooms sweep the jade steps.
Noon at the palace gate, a royal edict;
From behind a screen, an urgent call for a female clerk.

Poem 3

word no.	1	2	3	4	5	6	7
line no.							
紅 羅 袱 裹 建 溪 茶 1		O		X		O	@
侍 女 封 緘 結 出 花 2		X		O		X	@
斜 押 紫 泥 書 敕 字 3		X		O		X	
內 官 分 送 大 臣 家 4		O		X		O	@

Chien-ch'i tea[96] wrapped in red silk cloth;
A lady attendant seals and ties it with flower-like knots.
She stamps the imperial letters with a purple seal;
The eunuchs send them to various ministers.

Poem 8

word no.	1	2	3	4	5	6	7
line no.							
清 齊 秋 殿 夜 初 長 1		O		X		O	@
不 放 宮 人 近 御 床 2		X		O		X	@
時 把 剪 刀 裁 越 錦 3		X		O		X	
燭 前 閒 繡 紫 鴛 鴦 4		O		X		O	@

---

96. A place in Chien-ou County, Fukien, famous for its tea.

Lonely palace quarters of the Empress;[97] the evening is long.
A court lady still on duty stands by the royal bed;
Now and then her scissors cut out a piece of Yüeh silk.[98]
By candlelight she slowly embroiders it with mandarin ducks.[99]

Poem 9

	word no.	1	2	3	4	5	6	7
	line no.							
長 信 宮 門 待 曉 開	1		X		O		X	@
內 官 金 鎖 鎖 門 回	2		O		X		O	@
當 時 曾 笑 他 人 到	3		O		X		O	
豈 識 今 朝 自 入 來	4		X		O		X	@

I wait till dawn for the Palace of Trust[100] to open;
A eunuch, with a golden key, had locked the gate.
In the past I used to laugh at the others coming here.
How could I know that this morning it would be me?

Poem 13

	word no.	1	2	3	4	5	6	7
	line no.							
冰 簟 寒 多 夢 不 成	1		X		O		X	@
手 揮 羅 扇 撲 流 螢	2		O		X		O	@
長 門 永 夜 空 明 月	3		O		X		O	
風 送 西 宮 笑 語 聲	4		X		O		X	@

The bamboo mat so chilly, she is unable to sleep,
Strikes a wandering firefly with her silk fan.

---

97. The quarters of the Empress, known as the Ch'ang-ch'iu kung (The Palace of Prolonged Autumn). They were separate from the private apartment of the Emperor. At least in theory, the Empress spent every fifth night with him, returning to her own palace early in the morning. See Wei Hung 衛宏 (Han), *Han kuan chiu i* 漢官舊儀 (in *Ts'ung shu chi ch'eng ch'u pien* 叢書集成初編, Shanghai: 1935-37, no. 8111), pp. 9-10. Translation see Hans Bielenstein, *The Bureaucracy of Han Times* (Cambridge: 1980), p. 69.

98. Yüeh in Han times referred more generally to the far South including Kwangtung and Vietnam.

99. A symbol of conjugal affection.

100. Ch'ang-hsin Kung, the name of the Empress Dowager's quarters was located in the Ch'ang-lo Palace. Lady Pan (Pan Chieh-yü), consort of Emperor Ch'eng 成帝 (r. 33-7 B.C.) of the Former Han dynasty, is supposed to have composed a *fu* entitled Tzu-tao fu (Fu of Self-commiseration) after she had been slandered by her rival Chao Fei-yen 趙飛燕 (Lady Swallow) and relegated to the Ch'ang-hsin Palace to care for the Empress Dowager. See *Han shu, Chüan* 72, *Wang Chi chuan* 王吉傳, Chung hua shu chü ed. See also Miao, C. Ronald, *Studies in Chinese Poetry and Poetics* (San Francisco: 1978), p. 6.

An unending night at Long Gate Palace:[101]
A bright full moon lights the sky,
From the concubine's quarters,[102] the wind brings
   sounds of laughter and talk.

Poem 14

						word no.	1	2	3	4	5	6	7
						line no.							
綵	羅	帷	幕	紫	羅	茵	1		O		X		O	@
香	麝	霏	微	暗	襲	人	2		X		O		X	@
明	日	賞	花	留	玉	輦	3		X		O		X	
地	衣	簾	額	一	時	新	4		O		X		O	@

Rainbow-hued silk draperies, purple silk cushions;
A fine spray of hot musk seeps into the body.
Tomorrow His Majesty will view the flowers,
The rugs and curtains of royal carriage are being renewed.

Poem 15

						word no.	1	2	3	4	5	6	7
						line no.							
看	修	水	殿	種	芙	蓉	1		O		X		O	@
舁	下	羅	函	出	九	重	2		X		O		X	@
試	著	綵	衫	迎	詔	語	3		X		O		X	
翠	眉	猶	帶	睡	痕	濃	4		O		X		O	@

Orders to plant and tend the lotus of the pavilion pond;
A silk letter is sent from the palace.[103]
She strains into her formal costume to receive the royal edict,
Pencilled eyebrows still bearing the traces of sleep.

---

101. The Long Gate Palace (Ch'ang-men kung) was the name of a palace to which Empress Ch'en 陳, the wife of Emperor Wu of Han was relegated in 130 B.C. because she was barren. In desperation she asked Ssu-ma Hsiang-ju to compose a poem called Ch'ang-men fu 長門賦 (Fu of the Long Gate Palace) for her which is said to have restored the Emperor's compassion for her. See *Han shu*, chüan 65, *Tung-fang shuo chuan* 東方朔傳, Chung hua shu chü ed.
102. Hsi-kung 西宮 is a general term denoting the apartment of a royal concubine. See *Kung yang chuan* 公羊傳, *chüan* 11, Hsi kung 僖公 20th year, *Shih san ching chu shu* ed.
103. *Kujung* (Ch. *chiu-chung*) 九重: the nine divisions of the celestial sphere, *i.e.* the four cardinal points, the four intermediate points, and the centre called Heaven by Taoists, the Royal Palace by Koreans.

Poem 17

		word no.	1	2	3	4	5	6	7
		line no.							
新 擇 宮 人 直 御 床		1		X		O		X	@
錦 屏 初 賜 合 歡 香		2		O		X		O	@
明 朝 阿 監 來 相 問		3		O		X		O	
笑 指 胸 前 小 佩 囊		4		X		O		X	@

Newly chosen, a court lady enters the royal bed;
Silk screen drawn, she enjoys for the first time
    that fragrant union.
Next morning a head servant comes to ask questions;
Smiling, she points to the small purse of keepsakes
    over her bosom.

Poem 19

		word no.	1	2	3	4	5	6	7
		line no.							
西 宮 近 日 萬 機 煩		1		O		X		O	@
催 喚 昭 容 啟 殿 門		2		X		O		X	@
為 報 榻 前 持 燭 女		3		X		O		X	
漏 聲 三 下 紫 薇 垣		4		O		X		O	@

These days the Western Palace is busy;
A court lady[104] is urgently summoned to open the palace gate.
A court servant, holding a candle before the couch, reports.
The water-clock alerts the third watch in the Chami Garden.[105]

Commentary

Kung sa "Palace poem," belongs thematically to the so-called *kung-t'i shih* (Kor. *Kungch'e shi*) "Palace-style Poetry" or "Court Poetry." Its origin can be traced back to the courtly love poems of the Southern Dynasties. The convention of these love poems, especially the palace-style poetry, was for

104. *Soyong* 昭容 is an official title, given to the women of the court during the Chosŏn dynasty. Those who had relations with the King had the titles of *pin* 嬪, *kwiin* 貴人, *soŭi* 昭儀, *sugŭi* 淑儀, *soyong* 昭容, *sowŏn* 昭媛, etc. These ranged from the Upper First to the Lower Fourth court rank. Such women had no official duties at the court. The governess of the Upper Fifth rank and her inferiors down to the Lower Ninth rank had official duties at the court and could not be promoted above the Fifth rank.

105. Tzu-wei hsing (Kor. Chami sŏng) 紫微星 (The god of the Star). It is this star Tzu-wei which is supposed to be incarnated in the person of the Emperor. Hence the saying that when an Emperor has died: "A star has fallen from Heaven." The image of the star, the incarnation of the reigning emperor, was placed in the imperial palace.

the court poet, in composing love poems, to follow the appropriate device of rhetoric aesthetic rules and observe a strict poetic rule governing theme and approach toward the theme, as laid down by the literary circle of the court. For example, when the court poet wrote a love poem, his favoured subject was that of a woman in love, who is pining for her absent lover with unrelieved sorrow. This literary convention is derived from the ancient folk-songs of *Ch'u-tz'u* which are pervaded with melancholy stemming from the unfulfilled desire for love. A characteristic of the new poetic convention is that the female subjects are no longer the traditional merchant's wife or courtesan, as used to be the case with the old ballad songs, but are mostly aristocratic, graceful and glamorous women who live in luxury, often in palaces. It ensued that the palace-style poetry was centred on life in the palace, not only with its bewitching palace ladies, but including all the diverse matters relating to the court; such as court functions, architecture, objects of palace art, etc.

The poet describes these items in sensual and metaphorical detail. The woman portrayed is usually slenderly built, elegantly dressed and wearing expensive jewelry. He sets the stage as a luxurious boudoir, where nature is never too far away to make an effective contrast. There were two modes in which the court poets handled palace style poetry. The first was the creative imimtation of love songs drawn from the earlier *yüeh-fu* or folk-songs and reproduce them in much more refined lyrics, by applying a rigid rhetorical technique laid down by the literary circle of the court. The second was the description of the object or event as well as the most attractive fixtures of the palace, and the court lady in the daily life of the court was similarly described.

Nine poems of Nansŏrhŏn's *kung sa* out of twenty from her collection are translated and presented here with notes. All are written in seven-syllable *chŏlgu* with single rhyme in level tone occurring at the end of every first line and even numbered lines throughout. Of the nine, poems 1, 3, 8, 14, 15 and 19 follow the fixed tonal pattern of the level start and could be said to belong to the second category of the palace-style poetry. The songs are rather uninventive and impersonal, perhaps because palace-style poetry was regulated in order not to show directly any extremes of emotion by using rich and expressive words, but rather to prefer more noble expressions in elegant and polite terms, which were considered more aesthetically appealing.

In contrast, poems 9, 13 and 17 are written in the fixed tonal pattern of deflected start and belong to the first category. These poems deal with the court ladies, those either in or out of royal favour. It seems that Nansŏrhŏn deliberately used the deflected start to bring a general sad tone to these love poems. In poem 9 she expresses the humiliation of a court lady who was compelled to spend the night with her lord and was now waiting for the male servant to unlock the palace door.[106] Poem 13 is a courtly love song describing the unrelieved sadness and loneliness of a court lady who is pining for the royal favour. In poem 17 she depicts a union between a lord and a young and innocent court lady who was given a present of a bag of trinkets for a night's debauchery and the sacrifice of her maidenhood. Nansŏrhŏn's recognized skill in alluding to the relationship between the privileged and the non-privileged is well expressed in this poem, in elegant and subtle rhetoric.

The basic structural pattern of the palace-style poetry as set by the court poets was the tripartite form. This pattern, which had its origin in the poetry of second and third century China, was codified in *yulshi* late in the seventh century.[107] In consequence, a poem should first introduce the topic and then conclude with a personal reaction to it. This structural pattern continued to dominate the *koshi* and most of Nansŏrhŏn's palace songs follow it.

In poem 9, for example, she introduces the theme as elegantly as possible, beginning the first line with the Han palace name, which not only sounds graceful but also reminds her readers of the tragedy of the Lady Pan (see poem 9, note 100), thereby setting the sad tone in the poem. In the following two lines, Nansŏrhŏn describes the situation of a court lady who having spent the night with her lord is now anxiously waiting to leave the palace without being observed, (line 2). Finally, following the rules of the tripartite form she injects her own emotional response to the situation, reversing the witty tone of line 3 into a melancholic fatalism expressed in a simple and direct form of conclusion, in line 4.

This kind of poetic conclusion was often found in earlier forms of the tripartite pattern in which the poet used exclamatory endings, such as, "It makes me sad!" or "Who understands?" However, in poem seventeen the coda is attempted in a much more sophisticated manner. The poet's emotional or personal response to the topic described in the middle lines is neither clearly nor directly expressed, but is left open to the reader's own devices. Nansŏrhŏn simply sets a kind of scene which may act to bring about an emotional response in the reader. The reader is invited to come to some conclusion according to the note struck in the final line.

---

106. The entrance to the living quarters of the Royal family within the palace.
107. Stephen Owen, *The Poetry of Early T'ang,* New Haven, 1977, pp. 9-10.

Translation 18

"Wandering Immortals"

Form: 7-syllable *chŏlgu*

General Commentary

The following poems entitled *Yusŏn sa* belong thematically to the *hsüan-hsüeh* (Kor. *Hyŏnhak)* or metaphysical poetry. As observed in Chapter III, pt. 2 this kind of poetry was written during the Eastern Chin, but shortly after its heyday it lost favour in China. Scholars such as Stephen Owen and John Frodsham remind us that poetry, of which the main characteristic is neo-Taoistic speculation in highly abstract terminology, was considered distasteful by the Chinese. Thus, most of the *hsüan-hsüeh* poetry has been lost. Some poems however such as Kuo P'u's "Wandering Immortals" and various prose forms survived and became the fountain-head from which the themes of these poems were drawn.

In most of her poems on immortality Nansŏrhŏn expresses her conviction of the reality of an immortal world far removed from the harshness of her existence. Some however she uses more as allegorical symbols to express the heartfelt pain of her daily life and the desire to escape from a hostile world, than as expressions of her belief in the attainment of immortality. I have arranged these poems in three groups: in the first group immortals play an allegorical role; in the second group Nansŏrhŏn describes the kind of permanent bliss as corporeal. Finally, in the third group she describes the Taoist Heaven as the abode of immortals who nevertheless were collectively doomed since they, too, were bound to the Wheel of Life and Death. Professor Frodsham interprets this as Buddhist influence.[108]

The eighty-seven poems of *Yusŏn sa* are *akpu* style verse cast in seven-syllable *chŏlgu*. Of the poems which deal with the immortals in *akpu* form, some appear in Kuo Mao-ch'en's *YFSC* under "Matching Songs" in chapter 26, section 1. *Ch'i ch'u ch'ang* (Kor. *Kich'ul ch'ang)* and *Ching-lieh* (Kor. *Chŏngnyŏl)* by Emperor Wu of Wei; chapter 28, section 3. 11 poems of *Mo shang* (Kor. *Maeksang sang)*; chapter 37, section 12 three poems of *Pu ch'u hsia men hsing* (Kor. *Poch'ul hamun haeng)* and Ch'ü Yüan's *Li sao* (Kor. *Iso)* from *Ch'u z'u.*

---

108. See John Frodsham, *op. cit.,* pp. xli-xlii.

Yusŏn sa poems are written about mythological characters which appear in *Shan hai ching* (Kor. *Sanhae kyŏng*, The Book of Mountains and Seas),[109] *Mu t'ien-tzu chuan* (Kor. *Mok Ch'ŏnja chŏn*, The Travels of King Mu)[110] plus Kuo P'u's commentaries, the art of immortality in the *nei p'ien* of Ko Hung's *Pao-p'u tzu*,[111] Tung- fang Shuo's *Hai nei shih chou chi*, (The Accounts of Ten Continents), Ko Hung's *Shen hsien chuan*, Liu Hsiang's (77-6 B.C.) *Lieh hsien chuan* (The Accounts of Saints), *Han Wu Ti ku shih* (The Tales of Emperor Wu Ti), attributed to Tung-fang Shuo, Pan Ku, *Han Wu-ti nui chuan* etc.

---

109. *Shan Hai ching* (Kor. *Sanhae kyŏng*) 山海經 (The Book of Mountains and Seas) in eighteen volumes is a geographical compilation written in the form of fiction. It is a compendium of travellers tales which is regarded as a peerless treasury of early myths, legends and folk-tales, with accounts of miraculous phenomena in far-off regions. The tales are based on the assumption that every mountain and river of the known world has its guardian power, and by naming the offerings appropriate to their propitiation, implies the information to the power-seeking travellers—kings or wizards—who might feel disposed to make use of it. The myths here are not systematically arranged. The most important story in the work is believed to be that of *Hsi wang mu* (Kor. *Sŏwangmo*) 西王母 (Queen Mother of the West), which appears in *chüan* 2, *Hsi Shan ching* 西山經, because of its influence in the later period. See Kuo P'u ed., *Shan hai ching*, *Ku chin i shih* ed.

110. *Mu T'ien-tzu chuan*, in six books, records the imaginary progress to the far west of King Mu of the Western Chou dynasty on a chariot drawn by eight fine horses, and the offerings which he made to various powers in the course of it. The first five chapters describe this journey, while the last records the funeral of Lady Sheng 盛姬. The last chapter is considered to be originally a separate work. Unlike the *Hsi wang mu* in the Book of Mountains and Seas which portrays her as a monstrous being, she is described more like a human sovereign here. This work is said to have been found in a tomb of one of the Wei princes in 281, and was probably drawn up by someone during the late fourth or early third century B.C.E. There is a preface by Hsün Hsü of Chin, and a commentary by Kuo P'u. See *Mu T'ien-tzu chuan* plus Kuo P'u's commentary, *Ku-chin i-shih* ed.

111. *Pao-p'u tzu* consists of two chapters. The first chapter, Nei-p'ien 內篇, deals with studies for interior or personal application, principally that body of learning connected with becoming a Taoist immortal, although herbal medicines and semi-magical practices are also included. The second, Wai-p'ien 外篇 (Outer Chapters), deals principally with social and political philosophy and critical remarks on literature and the classics, and in general with the affairs of the society of which Ko Hung was a member—Jay Sailey, *The Master Who Embraces Simplicity* (San Francisco: 1978), p. ix.

Translation 18

"Wandering Immortals"

Form: 7-syllable *chŏlgu*

Poem 1

word no.	1	2	3	4	5	6	7
line no.							
千 載 瑤 池 別 穆 王　1		X		O		X	@
暫 教 青 鳥 訪 劉 郎　2		O		X		O	@
平 明 上 界 笙 簫 返　3		O		X		O	
侍 女 皆 騎 白 鳳 凰　4		X		O		X	@

> At the Emerald Pond of a Thousand Years,
>   she[112] farewells King Mu;[113]
> Then commands her oriole to visit Young Liu.[114]
> At dawn the flutes return to Skyland,
> Ladies-in-waiting all mounted on white phoenix.

Poem 7

word no.	1	2	3	4	5	6	7
line no.							
冰 屋 珠 扉 鎖 一 春　1		X		O		X	@
落 花 煙 露 濕 綸 巾　2		O		X		O	@
東 皇 近 日 無 巡 幸　3		O		X		O	
閒 殺 瑤 池 五 色 麟　4		X		O		X	@

112. *Hsi wang mu.*

113. Mu Wang (Kor. Mok wang 穆土, King Mu, 1001-946 B.C.) of the Chou dynasty is said in *Mu T'ien-tzu chuan,* to have visited a Hsi Wang mu who lived on K'un-lun Shan (Kor. Kongnyun-san 崑崙山, K'un-lun Mountains), and to have had an interview with her on the bank of the *Yao Ch'ih* (Kor. *Yoji* 搖池, Jasper Pool). It is recorded that he feasted with her at the P'an-t'ao Hui 蟠桃會 (The Feast of Peaches) which is attended by all classes of immortals. See *Mu T'ien-tzu chuan* plus Kuo P'u's commentary, *chüan 3, Ku-chin i-shih* ed.

114. Liu lang 劉郎 "Young Liu": some scholars take Young Liu not as an allusion to Emperor Wu of Han, Liu Ch'e 劉徹 but as one to Liu Ch'en, who, in a story, had a love affair with a goddess, but later failed to find his way back to the enchanted region, where he had met her. There are several reasons, however, for preferring to think that Emperor Wu is meant here. Firstly, in the story about Liu Ch'en, the fairy-land he visits is called T'ien- t'ai shan 天臺山 (T'ien-t'ai Mountain), not P'eng Mountain. Secondly, the poet Li Ho, who had considerable influence on Li Shang-in, used the phrase "Young Liu" in referring to Emperor Wu. Further, Li Shang-in himself refers to Emperor Wu in other poems concerned with secret love affairs. See James J. Liu, *The Poetry of Li Shang-yin,* (London:The University of Chicago Press, 1969), p. 63.

The pearl door[115] of the icy house is closed all Spring;
Smoky dew of falling flowers moistens the silk handkerchief.
These days the Eastern King[116] makes no royal tours;
At the Emerald Pond his multi-hued unicorn stands idle.

Poem 10

							word no.	1	2	3	4	5	6	7
							line no.							
煙	鎖	瑤	空	鶴	未	歸	1		X		O		X	@
桂	花	陰	里	閉	珠	扉	2		O		X		O	@
溪	頭	盡	日	神	靈	雨	3		O		X		O	
滿	地	香	雲	濕	不	飛	4		X		O		X	@

Fog blankets the emerald sky; the crane cannot return.
Under the shade of Cassia Flowers, the pearl doors are closed.
On the stream, all day long, divine rain falls;
Earth-drenching clouds of perfume, too damp and heavy to rise.

Poem 11

							word no.	1	2	3	4	5	6	7
							line no.							
青	苑	紅	堂	鎖	沈	漻	1		X		O		X	@
鶴	眠	丹	灶	夜	迢	迢	2		O		X		O	@
仙	翁	曉	起	喚	明	月	3		O		X		O	
微	隔	海	霞	聞	洞	簫	4		X		O		X	@

---

115. On *P'eng-lai shan* in the Eastern Isles, the houses are made of gold and silver. The birds and animals are all white and pearl and coral trees grow in great profusion. The flowers and seeds all have a sweet flavour. Those who eat them do not grow old nor die. There they drink of the fountain of life, and live in ease and pleasure. The Isles are surrounded with water which has no buoyancy, so it is impossible to approach them, They are inhabited only by the immortals, who have supernatural powers of transportation. See Wang Chia, *Shih i chi*, *chüan* 1 and *chüan* 10, *Ku chin i shih* ed.

116. Tung Wang-kung (Kor. Tong Wang-gong 東王公, The God of the Immortals). *T'ai-p'ing kuang chi* states that Tung Wang-kung is also called Mu Kung. The primitive elements solidified, remained inactive for a time, and then produced living beings. Life began with the formation of Mu Kung, the purest substance of the Eastern Air, and sovereign of the active male principle *yang*. His palace is in the misty heavens, violet clouds form its dome, blue clouds its walls. Hsien T'ung 仙童 (the Immortal Youth), and Yü Nü 玉女 (the Jade Maiden), are his servants. He is the registrar for all the Immortals, male and female. See *T'ai-p'ing kuang chi*, *chüan* 1.

Green Garden and Crimson Hall are secured;
A crane sleeps in the dispensary for immortality pill:[117]
  a long, long night.
An aged immortal rises at dawn and calls in the bright moon;
From the distant ocean of gossamer clouds, a flute sounds.

Poem 14

			word no.	1	2	3	4	5	6	7
			line no.							
閒 攜 姊 妹 禮 玄 都			1		O		X		O	@
三 洞 真 人 各 見 呼			2		X		O		X	@
教 著 赤 龍 花 下 立			3		X		O		X	
紫 皇 宮 里 看 投 壺			4		O		X		O	@

At leisure, with my two young sisters,
  I go to pay my respects in Heaven;
Immortals of the Three Islands call to see us.
I command the Scarlet Dragon to be harnessed amidst the flowers;
At the Purple Emperor's palace we watch the Dart and Bottle game.

Poem 44

			word no.	1	2	3	4	5	6	7
			line no.							
騎 鯨 學 士 禮 瑤 京			1		O		X		O	@
王 母 相 留 宴 碧 城			2		X		O		X	@
手 展 彩 毫 書 玉 字			3		X		O		X	
醉 顏 猶 似 進 清 平			4		O		X		O	@

The academician on a dolphin's back[118] pays a visit to Jade Capital;
Hsi Wang-mu gives a banquet for him at Jasper Castle.

---

117. See General Commmentary.
118. This refers to Li Po who was briefly a member of Han-lin Academy. Legend has it that Li Po was drowned in the river near Ts'ai-shih as he attempted, while drunk, to embrace the reflection of the moon in the water. This was further elaborated into a tale:
  "The moon that night was shining like day. Li Po was supping on the river when all of a sudden there was heard in mid-air a concert of harmonious voices, which sounded nearer and nearer to the boat. Then, the water rose in a great tumult, and lo! there appeared in front of Li Po dolphins which stood on their tails, waving their fins, and banners to indicate the way. They had come on behalf of the Lord of the Heavens to invite the poet to return and resume his place in the celestial realm. His companions on the boat saw the poet depart, sitting on the back of a dolphin while the harmonious voices guided the cortege... Soon they vanished altogether in the mist." — Obata Shigeyoshi, *op. cit.*, pp. 17-18.

He takes up the ornate brush and writes the word "Jade";
His drunken face just like it was when he composed the Odes,
  Ch'ing p'ing t'iao.[119]

Poem 87

			word no.	1	2	3	4	5	6	7
			line no.							
六 葉 羅 裙 色 曳 煙			1		X		O		X	@
阮 郎 相 喚 上 芝 田			2		O		X		O	@
笙 歌 暫 向 花 間 盡			3		O		X		O	
便 是 人 寰 一 万 年			4		X		O		X	@

A skirt with six strips of brocade trails along the clouds,
She calls young Juan and ascends to the iris fields;
Suddenly the lute music among the flowers stops;
In the temporal world ten thousand years have passed.

---

119. One day in spring Emperor Hsüan-tsung 玄宗 (r. 712-756) held a royal feast with Lady Yang Kuei-fei 楊貴妃 in the Pavilion of Aloes 沈香亭 where the peonies were in full bloom. When Li Po was summoned to capture for eternity the glory of vanishing hours, the poet was drunk. After cold water was poured on his face, he sobered and improvised three beautiful songs, *Ch'ing p'ing t'iao*, in praise of Yang Kuei-fei. See *CTS, chüan* 164 on Li Po, vol. 3, p. 1703.

Translation 19

"A Woman's Grievance"

Form: unclassified

Poem 1

							word no.	1	2	3	4	5	6	7
							line no.							
錦	帶	羅	裙	積	淚	痕	1		X		O		X	
一	年	芳	草	恨	王	孫	2		O		X		O	@
瑤	箏	彈	盡	江	南	曲	3		O		X		O	
雨	打	梨	花	晝	掩	門	4		X		O		X	@

Embroidered sash and silk skirt are wet with tears,
Every year fragrant plants lament a princely friend.[120]
On my lute I play to its end the South River Song;[121]
Showers of peach blossoms patter on the door, shut all day.

Poem 2

							word no.	1	2	3	4	5	6	7
							line no.							
月	樓	秋	盡	玉	屏	空	1		O		X		O	
霜	打	蘆	洲	下	暮	鴻	2		X		O		X	@
瑤	瑟	一	彈	人	不	見	3		X		O		X	
藕	花	零	落	野	塘	中	4		O		X		O	@

Autumn is over at the moonlit pavilion; its jade screen desolate.
Frost encrusts the reed island; wild geese roost for the night.
I play upon the jasper lute. No one sees me.
Lotus flowers drop into the pond.

Commentary

This poem which consisting of two stanzas and classified as miscellaneous in her collection, is, in fact, cast in the seven-syllable *chŏlgu* form. In the first stanza, the rhyme occurs at the end of each couplet in level tone and observes the fixed tonal pattern of a deflected start. In the second, the rhyme also

---

120. The word may be indebted to Hsieh T'iao's 謝朓 (464-499) "Wandering gentleman"; Green grass tendrils like silk, Trees abloom with red buds; Do not say, "I am not returning." When you do the fragrance will be gone. See Hsü Ling, *Yü-t'ai hsin yung* 玉臺新詠, *chüan* 10, Hsieh T'iao, vol. 2, p. 413, *Kuo hsüeh chi pen ts'ung shu* ed.

121. The south side of the Yangtze River. See commentary on p. 73-74 above.

occurs in level tone but follows the tonal pattern of a level start. Although the poem is treated as ordinary *shi*, the theme, that of the neglected wife, is undeniably in the *akpu* tradition. The sophisticated diction and complex symbolism used by the poet however indicate that the poem is far removed from the old *akpu* songs.

As a result of Confucian bias against eroticism, much love poetry tends to treat the subject in a less forthright manner by enhancing the sorrowful side of love, such as the loneliness of an ill-fated woman whose husband or lover has left her for one reason or other. Officials commonly went to provincial postings without their wives. The poet establishes an analogy between the world of nature and the human situation, and the juxtaposition is built on correspondences between the two worlds: the showers of peach blossoms tapping against the door which is shut all day, enhance the frailty and transience of the lonely woman behind a closed door, in the first stanza. In the second stanza, the poet creates the mood of Autumn in its final stage, thereby emphasizing the long intervals when the woman tires of waiting and the lotus flowers wither and fall.

Translation 20

"Autumn Plaint"

Form: unclassified

						word no.	1	2	3	4	5	6	7
						line no.							
絳	紗	遙	隔	夜	燈	紅	1		O		X		O	@
夢	覺	羅	衾	一	半	空	2		X		O		X	@
霜	冷	玉	籠	鸚	鵡	語	3		X		O		X	
滿	階	梧	葉	落	西	風	4		O		X		O	@

Screened by red gauze curtains,
the distant lamp burns into the night;
Waking from a dream, I find
silk bedspread half unfilled.
Icy frost: the orioles chatter in their cages.
Paulownia leaves, blown down by the west wind,
cover the steps.

Commentary

The poem is catalogued under "unclassified" in her collection. It is, however, a seven-syllable *chŏlgu* with single rhyme in level tone and follows the fixed tonal pattern of a "level start." This is another of her many plaintive poems. Though it is treated as ordinary *shi* rather than as *akpu* in form, its theme, that of the neglected wife, places it in *akpu* tradition, which could be traced back to "Matching Songs" (*chüan* 26-43) of *YFSC*.

The poem sets its scene in two places, inside and outside the lady's apartment, and a subtle contrast between these highlights the solitude. The red gauze and burning lamp in line 1 contrast with the freezing cold and falling leaves of the outside scene in line 4. A silk, half empty coverlet, in line 2 parallels the captive oriole in its fine cage. Finally, the abundance of falling leaves that fill the steps, in line 4, highlights the woman's loneliness. The poem is similar to Emperor Wu's (140- 87 B.C.), "The fallen leaves and the plaintive cicada," an elegy to the Emperor's concubine, as shown by the following extract;

落葉哀蟬曲

There is no rustle of silken sleeves,
Dust gathers in the Jade Courtyard.
The empty houses are cold, still, without sound.
The leaves fall and lie upon the bars of doorway
after doorway.

—Translated by Arthur Waley.

Translation 21

"Roaming Mt. Kwangsang in a Dream"

(Preface and Poem)

Preface

In the Spring of year *ŭryu* (1585) I was in mourning and stayed at uncle's.

In a dream I climbed up a mountain rising from the sea. The mountain was all beads and jade.

Peak upon peak of white beads from which a blue sheen sparkled and dazzled my eyes, until I was unable to see straight.

Rainbows cloud shrouded the peaks and the five rainbow colours looked beautifully fresh.

Several springs of red stones welled forth between the rocks of cliffs, making a sound of beads rolling.

Two ladies of about twenty years old and of rare beauty appeared.

One was wearing a jacket of scarlet and the other one was in green rainbow costume.

With golden bottle-gourd[122] in their hands, they approached me with light footsteps.

I followed the winding stream upwards. Strange plants and exotic flowers of unknown names were growing everywhere.

Phoenix, cranes, peacocks and kingfishers were flying, springing about from either side.

The forest was sending forth all kinds of sweet scents.

When I finally reached the top, the great seas of east and south joined with the sky, turning into one emerald colour.

The red sun had just risen and looked as if bathing in the wind.

The large pool at the summit was deep and clear. Green lotuses with big leaves were half withered by the frost.

The ladies said "This is Mt. Kwangsang, the best among the ten continents.[123]

---

122. There is a saying that whenever they compose poems, they drink from a bottle-gourd. The word gourd, Hu lu 壺蘆 in ancient Chinese can be written, 壺 Hu as in the Book of Odes. See Liu Ts'un-yen, *op. cit.*, p. 274.

123. Abode of the immortals. Emperor Wu of Han heard about the Ten Continents from Hsi Wang-mu and asked Tung-fang Shuo to describe these regions to him. Tung-fang Shuo is supposed to tell of the Ten Continents in *Shih chou chi* 十州記 (The Account of Ten Continents), a work probably of the Six Dynasties period attributed to him by later scholars. These continents are, Tsu 祖, Ying 瀛, Hsüan 玄, Yen 炎, Chang 長, Yüan 元, Liu 流, Sheng 生, Feng-lin 鳳麟, and Chu-k'u 聚窟. See *Shih chou chi* atributed to Tung-fang Shuo (154-93 B.C.) *Ku chin i shih* ed.

You must have links with the immortals; that is why you can come here.

Why not compose a verse to record it?" I declined but unsuccessfully.

Immediately I recited a verse. The two ladies clapped their hands, laughing with pleasure, saying, "Each stroke is the speech of an immortal."[124]

Suddenly a pack of red clouds came down from the sky on to the top of the peak. I was woken by the sound of a drum beat.

The air around my pillow was still shimmering.

Thinking that the atmosphere in which Li Po wrote the poem "His dream of Sky-land"[125] must have been like that, I simply recorded it.

The Poem reads:

					word no.	1	2	3	4	5
					line no.					
碧	海	浸	瑤	海	1		X		O	
青	鸞	倚	彩	鸞	2		O		X	@
芙	蓉	三	九	朵	3		O		X	
紅	墮	月	霜	寒	4		X		O	@

Sapphire Sea[126] flows into the Emerald Lake;[127]

Blue phoenix[128] mingles with the multicoloured one.

Twenty-seven lotus flowers.

Scarlet petals fall under the frosty moon.

---

124. 星星仙語 is used by Liu Yü-hsi 劉禹錫 (772-782) in his Pu-hsü tz'u 步虛詞 See *YFSC* *chüan* 78.

125. Refers to Li Po's poem called Meng yu T'ien-mu Ying (夢遊天姆留別, His dream of a Skyland: a Farewell Poem). In this poem Li Po describes his dream of visiting Mt. T'ien-mu "Foster Mother of the Skies" in Chekiang. T'ien-mu or Tou-mu 斗母 wears the Buddhist crown, is seated on a lotus throne, has three eyes, eighteen arms, and holds various precious objects in her numerous hands, such as a bow, spear, sword, flag, dragon's head, pagoda, five chariots, sun's disk, moon's disk, etc. She has control of the books of life and death, and all who wish to prolong their days worship at her shrine. In *chüan* 99 of *Feng shen yen i*, when Yüan Shih's 元始 mandate appointed the *Chin ling sheng mu* 金靈聖母 (The Holy mother of the Golden Spirit) to be the Tou mu (Mother of the Sagitarius) she had under her command a host of 84,000 evil stars. See Liu Ts'un-yen, *op. cit.*, p. 170.

126. Pi-hai (Kor, Pyŏkhae) 碧海: according to the *Accounts of Ten Continents*, Pi-hai is in Fu sang (Kor Pusang) 扶桑 which is on the far east coast of Eastern Sea. See *(Hai nei) shih chou chi*, Fu sang, *Ku chin i shih* ed.

127. *The Travels of King Mu* records the story of King Mu who drove his team of eight famous horses round the world. When he came to the K'ung-lun Mountains, *Hsi Wang mu* feasted him by the Emerald Pond.- *Mu T'ien-tsu chuan*, *chüan* 4, *Ku chin i shih* ed.

128. *Ran* 鸞: a mythical bird believed to be belonging to the phoenix family. Legend has it that the bird has five-coloured wings, resembles the peacock and sings melodiously.

Commentary

This poem like many *hanshi*, is prefaced by an introduction which describes the circumstances in which it was written. The poem has never been classified and is catalogued as miscellaneous in her collection. It is, however, a five-syllable *chŏlgu* which observes all the standard rules of this poetic form. The line length is constant five-syllable throughout. A single rhyme is in level tone at the end of the even numbered lines. The distribution of level and deflected tones follows a fixed pattern of a "deflected start." There is a caesura between the second and third syllables of every line.

The poetic introduction begins with a reference to Mt Kwangsan, one of the Ten Continents in the Eastern sea where immortals live. The poet describes her journey to a mountain which appears in her dream. Like the journey passages of the *Ch'u tz'u* her dream grows increasingly fantastic until it is shattered by the sound of a drum beat and she awakes. The following statement from the preface, "you must have links with immortals...," seemed to prove that Nansŏrhŏn believed in the reality of the Toaist heaven. Legend has it that Nansŏrhŏn, who devoted herself to *Hsien* Taoism, used to wear flowers when she recited the poems.[129] The last passage of the preface, "...thinking that the atmosphere in which Li Po, wrote his poem, 'His Dream of Skyland: a farewell poem' must have been like this..." reveals that she drew her inspiration from this particular poem. In his poem Li Po describes his dream of visiting Mt. T'ien-mu (Fostermother of the Skies) in Chekiang.

This is Nansŏrhŏn's only dated poem. It was written in the Spring of the 18th Year of King Sŏnjo's reign, i.e. 1585, just four years before her death. In its preface Nansŏrhŏn records:

> "In the spring of year 1585 I was in mourning and stayed at my uncle's. In a dream I climbed..."

At the end of this poem, Hŏ Kyun adds his commentary:

> "My sister died in the Spring of 1589. She was twenty-seven. 'The fall of twenty-seven scarlet lotus flowers' bears witness to her death."

But in his *Haksan ch'odam*, Hŏ Kyun also writes:

> "My sister used to write poems in her dreams, one of which reads: (he quotes the above poem). She died the following year..." (which makes 1586 and not 1589).

There is a discrepancy between Hŏ Kyun's two statements regarding the date of her death. If she died the year after she wrote the poem, as her brother says in his *Haksan ch'odam*, she should have died in 1586, and not in 1589, as he says in his commentary. I take his statement in *Haksan ch'odam* as a mistake.

---

129. See Ch'a Sangch'an 車相璨, Hŏ Nansŏrhŏn, *Pando sahwa wa nakt'o Manju* 半島史話와 樂土滿洲, 1942, p. 490.

This vividly colourful poem looks like a description of Nansŏrhŏn's death vision. It has been regarded as the poet's prophecy by the poet of her death, and Hŏ Kyun so interpreted it too, gaining her a reputation for uncanny clairvoyance. The timing is too precise to be sheer coincidence. The number of fallen scarlet lotus flowers is the same as her age at death. Since there are few pointers as to her state of health, other than the unverifiable belief that she might have been suffering from pulmonary tuberculosis, it is not possible to say whether she had a chronic illness.

Translation 22

"To my husband studying in the Kangsa Hall of Reading"[130]

Form: "Unclassified"

							word no.	1	2	3	4	5	6	7
							line no.							
燕	掠	斜	檐	兩	兩	飛	1		X		O		X	
落	花	撩	亂	撲	羅	衣	2		O		X		O	@
洞	房	極	目	傷	春	意	3		O		X		O	
草	綠	江	南	人	未	歸	4		X		O		X	@

Swallows perched in the angled eaves fly in pairs;
Blossoms falling pell mell tumble against silk dresses.
As I sit in the bedchamber gazing as far as the eye can see,
    feelings of love wound me;
The grass is green South of the River but you have not returned.

Commentary

This poem was originally not included in her collection, but in *Li tai nü tzu shih chi* under the title of Kyuwŏn "Woman's Grievance" and also in Yi Sugwang's *CBYS* with the title of 'Kibu kangsa toksŏ' (To my husband studying in the Kangsa Hall of Reading). This unclassified poem is a seven-syllable *chŏlgu* which observes its rules strictly, with a single rhyme in level tone at the end of the even numbered lines, and the tonal distribution following a fixed pattern of "deflected star."

The convention of the love-plaint poem, often cast in *yüeh-fu* style, goes back to the Chien-an poets of the Later Han. The theme of the neglected wife whose husband has left her, either because duty has called him away, or because he no longer cares for her, constitutes the bulk of "boudoir poetry" as mentioned earlier. This is one of Nansŏrhŏn's many poems in which she self-reflects as a lonely, neglected wife. Unlike most boudoir poetry written by men, who wrote generally of woman as a useless being outside the company of the man who yearns for her, the poem is inspired by her real-life experience and this is the tone of sincerity which breathes life into her poems.

---

130. Toksŏ-dang (The Reading Hall) where the civil officials on study leave used to read. It was established in 1426 in the 8th year of King Sejong's reign. Members were selected from those civil officials who were considered to be talented and virtuous scholars. By Royal appointment, the director of the Hall of Worthies, Pyŏn Kyeryang, conducted the selection at the Changŭi-sa Temple. The practice was abolished during the reign of King Sejo, but revived in 1491. In 1515 another Reading Hall was established in the present Tumo-p'o port and this one was called Tongho Toksŏ-dang 東湖讀書堂 because of its location.

Her husband spent a great deal of time away from home reading in Kangsa Hall in preparation for the Government Service Examination. Rumour abounds that his absences in order to study were often mere excuses to visit other women. Ironically he passed his Civil Service Examination in the year she died.

"Swallows fly in pairs" in line 1, "falling blossoms" in line 2 and "the distant man" in line 4 enhance the loneliness of the woman who stays in her boudoir and waits in vain for her husband throughout the Spring. The pun is involved in line 2 and 3 *ŭi* 衣 "clothes" in silk dress is homophonous with *ŭi* 意 "thought or feeling" in feelings of love: the beaten dress and the wounded feeling.

She expresses her own emotion through the persona of *Yüeh-fu* style poetry. Though the title follows that of normal lyric poetry, the poem is completely impersonal in setting aside her own voice and speaking in that of the forsaken wife, thus following the main stream of *yüeh-fu* tradition. It is understandable that the Chinese anthology includes this poem under the title of "Woman's Grievance," a traditional *yüeh-fu* theme.

Yi Sugwang points out that the reason for this poem not being included in her collection, is because of the eroticism it displays. The rigidity of Confucian society is clearly reflected in his remarks.

Translation 23

"Song of Lotus Gatherers"

Form: see commentary

				word no.	1	2	3	4	5	6	7
				line no.							
秋	淨	長	湖	碧	玉	流	1		X		O		X	@
菏	花	深	處	繋	蘭	舟	2		O		X		O	@
逢	郎	隔	水	投	蓮	子	3		O		X		O	
或	被	人	知	半	日	羞	4		X		O		X	@

The wide green lake in autumn, its streams like blue-green jade.
Buried amongst flowers, the magnolia boat is moored.
She meets her lover on the lake's far side and gives him lotus seeds;
Thinking someone may have seen, she has been bashful half the
day.

Commentary

This poem is not included in her extant Korean edition (see Chapter III, part 1, Derivation of Text of this book), and thus the modern edition catalogues it as "miscellaneous." The poem is a seven-syllable *chŏlgu* which has single rhyme at the end of the first, second and fourth line in level tone and observes the fixed tonal pattern of deflected start. Thematically, *Ch'aeryŏn kok* (Ch. *Ts'ai lien ch'ü*) belongs to the *akpu* song, dating back to the Liang dynasty. Of the twenty-seven *Wu yü* collected in *YFSC* under *Ch'ing shang ch'ü tz'u*, Chapter 50, the two earliest poems are written by Emperor Chien-wen of the Liang dynasty. *Ts'ai-lien ch'ü* is a Southern dynasty love song which portrays the lotus gatherer's life on the water, south of the River Yangtze. It is generally believed that when court poets of the Liang dynasty composed this song, they might have incorporated the theme of Chiang-nan, the Han folksong, as their background. There is a common link between these two songs.

Yi Sugwang, the author of *CBYS,* in which this particular poem of Nansŏrhŏn has been kept,[131] explains the reason for excluding the poem from her collection. The poem was regarded as referring to dissolute behaviour outside the Confucian code, and for this reason the Chinese who acquired her collection, which was originally published in China, began to tell stories about her. It looks as if the poem was included in the original manuscript, but was deliberately excluded later when the collection was printed in Korea.

---

131. Yi Sugwang *CBYS, Kwŏn* 14, *Munjangbu* 7, kyusu pp. 256-57.

Translation 22, "Kibu Kangsa toksŏ" had similar treatment and although kept in *CBYS*, was not in her collection.

This poem is a love song in a setting south of the River Yangtze, an area endowed with many beautiful lakes and rivers. Reference to the magnolia boat, in line 2, confirms this. Magnolia trees grow in abundance in this region and both boats and oars are made from its timber. The reference to lotus involves a pun: *lien* 蓮 (kor. *yŏn*, lotus seeds) is homonymic with *lien* 戀 (Kor. *yŏn*, to love) and is often used as a symbol of love in erotic poetry.

IV
Traditional Sources

"Talented females are also envious of fame;
About Nansŏrhŏn's personality opinions vary.
Twenty-seven lotus flowers: the fallen red blossoms,
Smiling, mark her return journey to Kwanghan Palace."[1]

When Shin Wi (1769-1847, styled Chaha) wrote this poetic dialogue, he was continuing the controversy about the authenticity of Nansŏrhŏn's work. The magnanimous view is to value her literary talent very highly and accredit the whole of her work as her own creation. Not quite so generous is the view that although her genius as a poet is to be recognized, it is arguable whether many of her poems were in fact her own work, or flowed from the pen of Hŏ Kyun. This latter speculation is moderated somewhat by its supporters, to the fall-back position of saying that if the majority of her poems were not by Hŏ Kyun, at least some of them were. The premise might be further extended to the degree that some of Nansŏrhŏn's poems are imitative of earlier Chinese poems, or were actually taken from Chinese collections of poems which were not widely read locally, and included in her collection.

Throughout the history of Korean literature, scholars have expressed divided opinions about Nansŏrhŏn's collected work and its authenticity. The origin of the view questioning authenticity may have arisen from several prejudices, such as the fact that Nansŏrhŏn was a female writer, whose work was overshadowing that of some male writers. It may have stemmed in part from the Korean poetic tradition of the time. Also telling against her was the downfall of her family, which contained some eminent writer-politicians,

---

1. *NSC*, p. 325.

with its members accused of treason, tried and convicted, resulting in their subsequent violent destruction.[2]

It has been argued at length that a few poems included in Nansŏrhŏn's collection were not her own compositions and this will be discussed later. It is the writer's opinion, however, that unless strong supporting evidence to the contrary can be produced, it is pointless to suggest that her poems are by anyone other than Nansŏrhŏn, to whom they have long been attributed.

The hostility of Chosŏn dynasty literati officials to any woman writer should be acknowledged. These officials maintained the strong view that women should be excluded from any attempt at intellectualism including reading classical Chinese and writing literary works in Chinese. In brief, they held that women should not be allowed to challenge the sphere of educated men. A woman such as Nansŏrhŏn, who was capable of writing excellent poems, possibly ones superior to those a male writer could produce, posed a definite threat to some literati officials. This naturally opened the way for destructive criticism of her collection, the result of which has been the longstanding controversy about its authenticity.

A statement made by Hong Taeyong (1731-1783, styled Tamhŏn) is an example of the official attitude of the time towards women writers, and the way in which their works were treated. Hong Taeyong went to Beijing as Military Attache and in this position had the opportunity to meet many Chinese literary figures. He recorded his discussion:

> "Women of our country should only read and write *han'gŭl* script. Writing poetry is not what a woman is supposed to do and even if she does, the poetry should be kept within the confines of the house and not be taken outside."

This invited a dialogue by Lang-kun[3] and he countered this criticism by replying:

> "Hŏ Kyun's sister, Kyŏngbŏn-dang (Nansŏrhŏn) of your country was well versed; her name has been included in the selections of Chinese poems. Isn't it very fortunate?"

Hong Taeyong retorted:

> "This lady's poems are excellent, but her virtue is a long way away from reaching the standard of her poems. Her husband is Kim Sŏngnip, whose talent and physical appearance are not praiseworthy. Also, there is a poem which says:
>
> > I wish I could part from Kim Sŏngnip in the world of men,
> > I could follow Tu Mu forever in the other world."

---

2. Nansŏrhŏn's second elder brother Hŏ Pong was sent to exile in Kapsan for three years and died there. Her younger brother Hŏ Kyun was convicted of treason and executed in 1618. See Chapter I, pp. 6-9 of this book.
3. P'ang T'ing-yun's 潘庭筠 courtesy name.

This brought a further response from Lan-kun:

> "A beautiful woman does not accompany an ugly husband. How could she be without resentment!"

Such a sentiment from a Chinese writer-painter might have concluded the dialogue, but Hong Taeyong had the final word:

> "In their spare time from woman's work, they may study literature and history to learn women's precepts and the cultivation of feminine virtues! This is what women are supposed to do. To cultivate fine literature and eventually acquire fame, is not the right way (to act)." [4]

While Hong Taeyong grudgingly acknowledges Nansŏrhŏn's literary talent, he seems distressed that her literary excellence in this respect is so patently expressed in her poems about love and the resentment of a neglected woman. His overriding concern, however, is that her works were published rather than being kept within the confines of the home, thus allowing her prowess as a poet to reach a wide circle of readers.

There is voluminous evidence available to illustrate the very negative attitudes of the literati officials towards women writers and how their literary activites were curbed during the Chosŏn dynasty. On the other hand, there is Hŏ Kyun, a scholar who not only acknowledged that women writers did exist, but who actually offered them encouragement to continue writing. Hŏ Kyun's account reads:

> "In our country there have been very few women who were able to write verse. Is that because of the saying—women should be only concerned with cooking food? Going beyond that and trying to write literature is not proper! Yet we can find, from Chinese literature, that during the T'ang dynasty there were more than twenty women who were able to produce elegant verses. Recently, however, we have more and more female writers such as Kyŏngbŏn, who has talent like an immortal. Similarly, as the number of women writers increases, so it is with the variety of their literary interests, to the extent that these can no longer be counted on the fingers. Even in comparison with the T'ang poetesses, our country has no reason to be ashamed." [5]

Despite the high-handed attitude by the literati officials, it is interesting to note that women writers flourished, though the prejudice against them persisted over the centuries. Perhaps the most important fact to remember here, is that by and large, commentators on Nansŏrhŏn's work have applauded her as the best female poet of the Chosŏn dynasty.

---

4. Yi Tŏngmu 李德懋, *Ch'ŏngjanggwan chŏnsŏ* 靑莊館全書, *kwŏn* 63, *ch'ŏnae chigisŏ* on p'iltam, *op. cit*, p. 506.
5. *HKCS*, p. 478.

I have divided the traditional sources into two parts, affirmative and negative, to support both arguments, following which a conclusion is drawn. Some accounts may not be directly related to the controversial content, but they are included here, simply to introduce, as far as possible, the traditional sources available, which are considered essential to the study of Nansŏrhŏn's work.

A. The Affirmative Sources

Source 1   Hŏ Kyun, in *Sŏngso pokpugo* chapter 3, *Pu*, Section 1, part 2, *Sa*,

Source 2   _____, *Haksan ch'odam*, written 1593,

Source 3.1   Yu Sŏngnyŏng's epilogue to Nansŏrhŏn's collection,

Source 3.2   _____, *Sŏae sŏnsaeng pyŏlchip*, *kwŏn* 4, *Chapchŏ*, on talented female poets,

Source 4   Extract from Nam Yongik, *Hogok shihwa*,

Source 5   Extract from Hwang Hyŏn, *Maech'ŏn chip*,

Source 6   Extract from P'eng Kuo-tung's *Chung-Han shih shih*.

Chapter 1 (Life of Hŏ Nansŏrhŏn) includes a discourse on Sources 1 to 3.1, and, therefore, to avoid repetition they are not repeated here. These sources are the accounts of commentators who have not directly concerned themselves with authenticity, their writing illustrating their belief in Nansŏrhŏn's work as being beyond plagiarism.

B. The Negative Sources

Source 7   Extract from Ch'ien Chien-i's *Lieh ch'ao shih chi*.

Source 8   Extract from Yi Sugwang's *Chibong yusŏl*.

Source 9   Extract from Kim Man'jung's *Sŏp'o mamp'il*.

Source 10   Extract from Chu Yi-tsun's *Ming shih tsung*.

Source 11   Extract from Shin Hŭm's *Ch'ŏng ch'ang yŏndam*.

Source 12.1   Extract from Yi Tŏngmu's *Ch'ŏngjanggwan chŏnsŏ*.

Source 12.2   _____, *Ch'ŏngbirok*.

Source 13   Extract from Pak Chiwŏn's *Yŏrha ilgi*.

The negative sources are drawn from the accounts of those who maintain that some or most of her works are taken from Chinese poems.

A. The Affirmative Sources

Source 1   Extract from *Sŏngso pokpugo*, chapter 3, *Pu*,
                  section 1, part 2, *Sa*.

Source 2   From *Haksan ch'odam* by Hŏ Kyun, written 1593.

Source 3.1   Yu Sŏngnyong's epilogue to Nansŏrhŏn's collection.

Source 3.2   From *Sŏae sonsaeng pyŏlchip*, *kwŏn* 4, *Chapchŏ*,
                  on talented female poets:[6]

"In recent years there have been several talented female poets. One of them is Miss Hŏ, styled Nansŏrhŏn, the daughter of the Governor Yŏp of Kyŏngsang Province. When she grew up she married Kim Sŏngnip. Among many females, she had outstanding talent. I record two of her poems here:

"A Woman's Grievance"
Embroidered sash and silk skirt are wet with tears,
Every year fragrant plants lament a princely friend.
On my lute I play to its end the South River Song;
Showers of peach blossoms patter on the door, shut all day.
Autumn is over at the moonlit pavilion; its jade screen desolate.
Frost encrusts the reed island; wild geese roost for the night.
I play upon the jasper lute. No one sees me.
Lotus flowers drop into the pond.

Her poems are very much like poems of the T'ang period. I have recorded two poems, but there are many others. She died at twenty–some years."

Source 4   Extract from Nam Yongik, *Hogok shihwa*.[7]

"People sometimes say, when referring to Nansŏrhŏn's poems that they are the work of Kyun himself, which he passed off under a false name to hoodwink the public. Her rhymes however are superior to those to which Hagok (Hŏ Pong) or (Hŏ) Kyun could aspire. At Okdang Hall, I once saw a book titled *Hsüan shih*. Nansŏrhŏn's collection was included at the end of that book. She could compete with all the immortals banished from Heaven (all the great poets of China.)"

He went on to say:

"His (Kyun's) sister's, 'The Palace Songs,' one hundred stanzas[8] are really exquisite."

---

6. Yu Sŏngnyong, Sŏae munjip, op. cit., p. 404.
7. Hong Manjong, *Shihwa ch'ongnim*, *op. cit.*, pp. 387-416.
8. There are only 20 stanzas in her collection.

Source 5   Extract from Hwang Hyŏn, *Maech'ŏn chip*.[9]

"On reading the poems written by the poets of Chosŏn dynasty: poem 10"

> Three precious trees of Ch'odang family,[10]
> The talent of the first rank befitting an immortal belongs to
>   Kyŏngbŏn.[11]
> She knew a long life in this world would be difficult;
> Lotus flowers look lonely with a trace of the frosty moon."

Source 6   Extract from P'eng Kuo-tung's *Chung-Han shih shih*.[12]

"The reason that the poems of Nansŏrhŏn are similar to those of Li Meng-yang; Ho Ching-ming; Wang Shih-cheng and Li P'an-lung is because she studied the Complete Works of Tu Fu (*Tu kung pu chi*). [13] There were also the collections written by both Hsien-chi (Li Meng-yang) and Chung-mo (Ho Ching-ming) in Korea. During the Wan-li period Li Shih-fang accompanied envoys to Korea and circulated Yen-chou chi.[14] For such reasons, it is possible they used these poems as a model and framework for their own writings. Chu obviously did not read *Yu ssu shih hua*[15] and thus could not realize that the works of the Former and Latter Seven Masters were popularly emulated. When I read Nansŏrhŏn's poems, her proudly unbending and bright and clear quality, surpasses her brother's talents and she could be described as peerless. No one should suspect forgery."

B. The Negative Sources

Next are the accounts by those who maintained that some of her works are taken from Chinese poems. Few however give accurate information.

Source 7   Extract from Ch'ien Ch'ien-i's (1582-1644, styled:
            Mu-chai) *Lieh ch'ao shih chi*.[16]

"Hŏ Kyŏngbŏn, styled Nansŏl was a Korean woman whose elder[17] brothers, both Pong and Kyun, attained the highest marks in the Government Service

---

9. Hwang Hyŏn 黃玹, *Maech'ŏn Shijip* 梅泉詩集, vol. 2, on Tok kukcho chegashi 讀國朝諸家詩.
10. Ch'odang is Hŏ yŏp's (Nansŏrhŏn's father) penname, thus Ch'odang family refers to Nansŏrhŏn's family.
11. Kyŏngbŏn: Nansŏrhŏn's courtesy name.
12. P'eng Kuo-tung, *Chung-Han shih shih*. Shin Hoyŏl tr., *Han- Chung shisa* 韓中詩史 2 vols. (Seoul: Taehan Min'guk Kongboshil, 1960), vol. 2, p. 74.
13. *Pullyu Tugongbu shi ŏnhae:* See pp. 7-8, 20 above.
14. Collected works of Wang Shih-chen, styled Yen-chou Shan jen. See Chu Yi-tsung, *op. cit.*, *chüan* 46, *Ming shih chi shih* 明詩紀事, 1.
15. Poetic discourse of Chang Kuo-wei 張國維 (Ming, styled Yu-ssu). See *ibid.*, *chüan* 74, Hsiao t'ien chi nien, 3.
16. Ch'ien ch'ien-i, *Lieh ch'ao shih chi*. Han Ch'iyun 韓致奫 (1765-1814, styled Ogudang), *Haedong yŏksa* 海東繹史, 2 vols, photo-reprint ed. (Seoul:1974), vol. 2, pp. 457-59.

Examination. At the age of eight she wrote a piece of prose called, "Inscriptions on the Ridge Pole of the White Jade Pavilion in Kwanghan Palace." (It is said) her talent surpasses that of her two elder brothers. She married Kim Sŏngnip, but it was not a happy union and her husband was later killed in battle.[18] Eventually she became a Taoist nun."[19]

A Chinese envoy to Korea, Cu Chih-fan (Styled Lan-yu) of Ching-lin acquired Nansŏrhŏn's collection, and when he returned to his homeland brought her work back with him. It was circulated widely in China. Liu Ju-shih (mistress of Ch'ien Ch'ien-i) said that Sister Hŏ's poetry and prose are as elegant as falling flowers and please all tastes. It was when I read Nansŏrhŏn's "Wandering Immortals," with lines like, "It has been ten thousand years in the world of man 便是人寰一萬年"(last line of poem 87) and "Welcome the young Immortal Master at Jasper Castle 碧城激取小茅君" (Last line of poem 4) that I realized they were the lines of Ts'ao T'ang.[20] A line from "Song of the Willow Branches 楊柳枝詞," which reads, "You do not pull willow branches off to welcome people, but to farewell them 不解迎人 解送人" (last line of poem 5), is that of P'ei Shuo (*Chin-shih* 906).[21] The lines from "Palace Poems," such as, "The rugs and curtains are changed at once 地衣簾額一時新"(last line of poem 14), are completely taken from a poem of the same name, by Wang Chien[22] "In the past I used to laugh at the others coming here當時曾笑他人倒: How could I know that this morning I myself would come in 豈識今朝自入來" (last two lines of poem 9), are taken from a poem of the same name by Wang Yai (765?-835?, styled Kuang-chin).[23]

Poem 3 of the "Palace Song," which reads:

> "Chien-hsi wrapped in red silk cloth 紅羅袱裹建溪茶;
> A Lady attendant seals it and ties it with flower like knots 侍女緘結出花.
> She stamps the imperial letters with a purple seal 斜押紫泥書勅字;
> The eunuchs send them to various ministers 內官分送大臣家."

---

17. Hŏ Kyun is Nansŏrhŏn's younger brother, and thus this statement is not correct.
18. *Imjin waeran* 壬辰倭亂, Japanese Invasion of Korea, 1592-98.
19. This is mistaken information. See pp. 117-118 below.
20. The lines referred to in *Lieh ch'ao shih chi* as Ts'ao T'ang's are as follows;
　　不過激取小茅君, and not 碧城 激取小茅君 (a); 便是人寰一萬年 instead of 便是人間一萬年 (b).
(a) Last line of Yu hsien tz'u 遊仙詞 poem 20.
(b) Last line of Hsio yu hsien tz'u 小遊仙詞 poem 80. See *CTS*, vol. 19, pp. 7436-7450.
21. P'ei Shuo's poem entitled "Willow (柳)," See *CTS*, vol. 21, p. 8269.
22. Last line of Wang Ch'ien's "Palace Songs (宮詞)", poem 40. See *CTS*, vol. 10, p. 3442.
23. Last two lines of Wang Yai's "Palace Songs," poem 9, from which Nansŏrhŏn is supposed to have taken is as follows:
　　誰知會笑他人處
　　今日將身他人來 See *CTS*, vol. 11, p. 3878.

is a combination of two lines, one each of Wang Chung-ch'u (Wang Chien) and Wang' Ch'i-kung (Wang Kuei), which reads, 黃金合裏盛紅雲[24] and 內庫新函進御茶[25] respectively and which have been jumbled-up and intermingled. The line of poem number four, which reads, 閒廻翠首依簾立 却對君王設隴西, is also taken from Wang Chung-ch'u's line, 數對君王憶隴山[26] Two lines from, "Written to Rhyme Pattern of Sung of the Courtesan's Quarters," which read, "She looks at her freshly powdered face in the mirror 新粧滿面猶看鏡; troubled by the remnants of a dream, she is reluctant to come down 殘夢關心懶下樓," are those from the Yüan poet Chang Kuang-p'i's (Chang Yu, 1289-1371) poem called, "Without Title."[27]

Wu Tzu-yü's (Wu Ming-chi) *Cha'o hsien shih hsüan* (Anthology of Korean Poems),[28] includes three hundred poems of "Wandering Immortals" by Ma Hao-lan (Ma Hung) of the Ming dynasty.[29] A look at the Hsi hu chih yu "West Lake Miscellany,"[30] shows that other lines have been taken and included in Nansŏrhŏn's poems. Poems with such titles as "Willow Branches" and "Bamboo Branches," which are part of her collection, are all adapted from identical titles of old poems circulated in Korea. People in Korea thought the book was rare (and could not be found easily elsewhere), so they wanted to keep the poems in it as their own. When the Chinese literati, ever searching for something exotic, saw these poems by a foreign woman, they were agreeably surprised and thought very highly of them. They did not enquire into the authenticity of her work.

Madam Fang of T'ung ch'eng collected poems and compiled "*A History of Poetry.*" In her poetic critique she succinctly ridicules the poems written by Madam Hsu, with the words,

"In spite of her ignorance, she tries to gain a reputation." Ladies in Wu Chung thought that Sister Ho's poetry was not simple enough for them to understand what she is talking about. I was ordered by my master to collate the poetry written by women. Whenever I thought up new ideas about poetry, I put them down on

---

24. The first line of Wang Chien's "Palace Songs," poem 67. See *CTS* , vol. 10, p. 3443.
25. 王岐公: Wang Kuei 王珪 (1019-1085) of Sung dynasty was conferred the title of Lord of Ch'i-kuo 岐國公. For the line quoted above, see *Hua yang chi* 華陽集 vol. 1, *chüan* 6, p. 61. *Tsung shu chi ch'eng* 叢書集成, no. 1912.
26. The last line of Wang chien's "Palace Songs," poem 86. See *CTS* , vol. 10, p. 3444.
27. The two lines quoted above, see *K'o hsien lao jen chi*, vol. 4, *chüan* 4, p. 79. *Ssu k'u ch'üan chu chen pen ch'u chi* ed 四庫全書珍本初集.
28. *Ch'ao-hsien shih hsüan* is not included in *Chung Kuo ts'ung shu tsunglu* 中國叢書綜錄, and may have been lost. However, Ch'ien Ch'ien-i's, *Chiang yun lou shu mu* 絳雲樓書目 records the following fact, "During Wan-li period a reinforcement army was sent to Korea. Wu Ming-chi of Ts'eng-chi followed the army to P'yŏngyang and collected poems from that county (Korea). Hŏ Kyun, who is the most well known Korean literary man, wrote the postscript." See Ch'ien Ch'ien-i, *Chiang yun lou shu mu*, (Taipei:1969), *chüan* 3, p. 156.
29. See Ch'ien Chien-i, *Lieh ch'ao shih chi hsiao ch'uan, op. cit.*, vol. 1, p. 196-97. It records that there are about 100 poems of "Wandering Immortals" included in his collection, entitled *Hua ying chi* 花影集. *Hua ying chi* is not included in *Chung kuo ts'ung shu tsung lu* and is possibly lost.
30. *Hsu hu chi yu* is not included in the *Chung kuo ts'ung shu tsung lu* and is possibly lost.

paper. The poems I have included here are selected from *Chao hsien shih hsüan*, I have chosen about one-fifth of her poems from it. I tried to find the original sources, but failed to find all of them. Therefore, the reader should be wary."

Source 8   Extract from Yi Sugwang's *Chibong yusŏl*.[31]

"Nansŏrhŏn, Miss Hŏ, was the wife of Chŏngja[32] Kim Sŏngnip. She was the foremost among the literary women of recent times. She died very young and left a collection. During her lifetime she was unable to experience conjugal harmony, and therefore wrote a great deal of poems dealing with resentment. One is entitled, "Song of the Lotus Gatherers" which reads:

> The wide green lake in autumn, its streams like blue-green jade.
> Buried amongst flowers, the magnolia boat is moored.
> She meets her lover on the lake's far side and gives him lotus seeds;
> Thinking someone may have seen, she has been bashful half the day.

Rumours about her were spread by the Chinese man who acquired her collection. One such source is the poem she sent to her husband Sŏngnip when he was a young man studying at the Kangsa Hall of Reading:

"To My Husband in the Kangsa Hall of Reading"
> Swallows perched in the angled eaves fly in pairs;
> Blossoms falling pell mell tumble against silk dresses.
> As I sit in the bedchamber gazing as far as the eye can see,
>   feelings of love wound me;
> The grass is green South of the River but you have not returned.

These two poems were criticized by the people as referring to dissolute behaviour and, therefore, are not included in the collection. One poem in her anthology, "Song of Colouring Nails with Touch-me-not Balsam" was undoubtedly taken wholly from the lines of a poem by a Ming dynasty poet and re-arranged. Her version reads:

> 拂鏡火星流夜月
> 畫眉紅雨過春山 [33]

---

31. *CBYS*, pp. 256-57.
32. *Chŏngja* 正字 (The Ninth Counsellor of the Office of the Special Counsellors).
33. Her lines read: 時把彩毫描却月
> When I draw my crescent eyebrows with a brush,
> 只疑紅雨過春山
> It is also like scarlet raindrops passing by the spring mountains.

Two lines provided by Yi Sugwang are not quite the same as those of Nansŏrhŏn.

Among the poems of "Wandering Immortals," two are poems by Ts'ao T'ang of T'ang dynasty.[34] One stanza of "Escorting Court Lady to the Taoist Temple" is that of the Ming dynasty poet T'ang Chen.[35] Besides these, *yüeh-fu* style "Palace Songs" and many others were taken from old style verse (*koshi*).[36] The Third Minister of the Board (*ch'amŭi*) Hong Kyŏngshin and the Section Chief of the Board (*chŏngnang*) Hŏ Chŏk from the same family always said that with the exception of two or three, the rest of the poems in Nansŏrhŏn's collection are fakes. People also said that the prose piece entitled, "Inscriptions on the Ridge Pole of the White Jade Pavilion in the Kwanghan Palace," was written by Hŏ Kyun and Yi Chaeyŏng and not by Nansŏrhŏn."

Yi Sugwang recognized Nansŏrhŏn's talents and considered her as the cleverest female poet of that time, but thought it a pity that Hŏ Kyun's mismanagement of his sister's surviving works caused suspicion among readers. In his treatment of the authenticity of her work, however, Yi Sugwang based his argument on material provided by Ch'ien Ch'ien-i in his *Lieh Ch'ao shih chi.*[37]

Source 9   Extract from Kim Manjung's (1637-1692, styled Sŏp'o) *Sŏp'o mamp'il.*[38]

"Nansŏrhŏn's verses are derived from the poetry of Yi Son'gok (Yi Tal) or her brother Hagok (Hŏ Pong). Though her learning never reached the standard achieved by Okpong (Paek Kwanghun) and the others (meaning the Three T'ang Talents of Korea), she was far cleverer than them and was the only female writer in Haedong (ancient name for Korea). It is a pity that her younger brother Hŏ Kyun selected some of the beautiful but unfamiliar verses written during the Yüan and Ming dynasties of China and included them in Nansŏrhŏn's collection, publishing them as if they were her compositions, in order to add to her reputation. Although it was possible to deceive the Korean readers, yet the works were carried back to China! This is just like a robber stealing a cow or a horse to sell back to the village from which they came. I must say this is extremely stupid. Unfortunately Hŏ Kyun met Ch'ien Mu-chai (Ch'ien Ch'ien- i) whose two eyes were like those of Lord T'ao[39] who noticed the government owned willow tree in

---

34. One of them, the last stanza of "Wandering Immortals" is also quoted in *Lieh ch'ao shih chi* as Ts'ao Tang's work.
35. See Source 7 above.
36. *Ibid.*
37. For the present writer's assessment of this extract, refer to Source 7 of this chapter.
38. See Kim Manjung, *Sŏp'o mamp'il, op. cit.*, p. 627-628.
39. T'ao K'an 陶侃 (259-334, styled Shih-hsing 士行. While he held the position of Grand Warden of Wu-ch'ang (Hupei) a great number of willow trees were planted. A resident stole one of the trees and planted it in his yard. When T'ao K'an was passing by the house he noticed the tree and questioned the man, saying, "Have you stolen the government's willow?" The man is supposed to have confessed to the theft. See Liu Yi- ching 劉義經 (403-444), *A New Account of the Tales of the World,* tr. Richard B. Mather, (Minneapolis:1976), p. 575.

a private backyard in Wu ch'ang,[40] and uncovered the deception, thereby bringing great shame upon the perpetrator. What a pity!"

"Since ancient times there have been very few who gained a reputation comparable with those of long ago, like Hsieh Tao-yun[41] or Lady Pan. As to Miss Hŏ's talent: it was sufficient to make her the cleverest woman of her time. It is, however, really sad that, by this self imposed trouble, people were led to doubt each section of her work and search for the defects in each of her verses. Nansŏrhŏn also gave herself the title Kyŏngbŏn-dang which was taken out of respect for Madam Fan, who, together with her husband is said to have become an immortal."

The source does not refer to any single poem which may have been plagiarised, although it does denote the periods in which the original poems may have been produced. The verses written during the Yüan and Ming dynasties seem to suggest that the original poems were by Chang Kuang-pi of the Yüan and Ssu-ma Hsiang ju of the Ming dynasties, as Ch'ien Ch'ien-i points out in his *Lieh ch'ao shih chi*.

Source 10　　　Extract from Chu Yi-tsun's *Ming shih tsung*,
　　　　　　　"An Anthology of Ming Poetry."[42]

"Kyŏngbŏn styled Nansŏl was the sister of Pong and Kyun and married to Kim Sŏngnip. After Sŏngnip died for his country, she finally became a Taoist nun.[43] She left a collection. Kyŏngbŏn at the age of eight wrote, "Inscriptions on the Ridge Pole of the White Jade Tower in Kwanghan Palace." Her talent was superior to that of her brothers, Pong and Kyun. The following poems from her collection were acquired by Chuang-yuan[44] Chu Chih-fan (fl.1595) of Chin ling, who was an envoy[45] to Korea. He returned home with the book[46] and it eventually circulated widely in China. Ch'en Wo-tzü said that Miss Hŏ was taught by Yi Tal and both of their verses are expressed in the High T'ang style. The fact that a woman of a foreign country is so well versed (in Sino-Korean) shows that the teaching of this country's literature is indeed far-reaching. Criticism of the poetry, however, reveals that many of this woman's poems lack authenticity...When I read Kyŏngbŏn's (Nansŏrhŏn) poems her poetic syntax was in the same style as that of the Seven Masters of the Chia ching period. There have never been examples, like this, of

---

40. Wu-ch'ang commandery. Former capital near modern O-ch'eng in Hupeh.
41. Hsieh Tao-yün, (Second half, fourth cent.). Daughter of Hsieh I, elder sister of Hsieh Hsüan, and wife of Wang Ning-chih. She was a very prolific poet but nothing has survived of her work. See Liu Yi-ching, *op.cit.*, p. 529.
42. Chu Yi-tsun, *Min shih tsung*, *chüan* 95, pt. 2, Colonies, pt. 2, 1705 ed., vol. 30.
43. As Pak Chiwŏn pointed out in his *Yŏrha ilgi*, this is mistaken information. See pp. 115-116 below.
44. *Chuang-yüan:* highest graduate of Hanlin Academy.
45. Chin ling: Name for Nanking
46. See p. 30-31 above.

cultural contracts between the two countries. How could the similarity exist (without such contact)? I cannot but suspect that it may be forgery."

Source 11   Extract from Shin Hŭm's (1566-1628, styled Sangch'on) *Ch'ong ch'ang yŏndam.*[47]

"A daughter of Hŏ Ch'odang (Hŏ Yŏp) and a wife of Kim Sŏngnip... Her works are similar to those written by The Four Talents of T'ang. But her collection includes poems taken from ancient works, including more than half of the "Wandering Immortals." I once read two stanzas of her modern style verse, "Written to Rhyme Pattern of Sung of the Courtesan's Quarters":

> She looks at her freshly powdered face;
> Troubled by the remnants of a dream,
> she is reluctant to come down

These are lines taken from an ancient poem.[48] Some people also say that her brother had stolen them from the poems which are not widely read by the people and included them in her collection, in order to increase her reputation. There is little worse than this."

Shin Hŭm's argument along these particular lines has already been discussed in pp. 107-110 of this chapter on Source 7.

Source 12.1   Extract from Yi Tŏngmu's *Ch'ŏngjanggwan chŏnsŏ.*[49]

Lan-kung (P'an T'ing-yun) said, "Hŏ Kyun's sister, Kyŏngbŏn-dang of your country was well versed; her name has been included in the selections of Chinese poems. Isn't it very fortunate!"

Tamhŏn Hong Tae-yong (1731-1783) replied, "This lady's poems are excellent, but her virtue is a long way from reaching the standard of her poems. Her husband is Kim Sŏngnip whose talent and physical appearance is not praiseworthy. And also there is a poem which says:

> I wish when I part from Kim Sŏngnip in the world of men,
> I could follow Tu Mu forever in the other world.

Lan-kung said, "A beautiful woman is accompanied by an ugly husband. How could she be without resentment."

Hyŏngam (Yi T'ŏngmu) said, "I was once told that Kyŏngbŏn is not a pen-name which Nansŏrhŏn took but one insincere people sneeringly gave her." Tamhŏn

47. Shim Hŭm, *Ch'ŏng ch'ang yŏndam.* Hong Manjong, *Shihwa ch'ongnim op. cit.,* kwŏn 2, p. 226.
48. Two lines, however, are clarified in *Lieh ch'ao shih chi* as a Yüan poet, Chang Kuang-pi's.
49. Yi Tŏngmu, *op. cit.,* vol. 3, pt. 2, p. 506.

couldn't defend it in time. In Chinese books Hŏ Kyŏngbŏn and Nansŏrhŏn are separated as two different people. Those books also record, "Her husband died for his country during the Japanese invasion and Miss Hŏ became a Taoist for the rest of her life". That was also a grave mistake. If Lan-kung compiles a poetic discourse and includes this statement of Tamhŏn, Nansŏrhŏn will be an extremely unfortunate person. Also if one tries to point out the flaws, none of her poems, like those of Liu Ju-shih (mistress of Ch'ien Ch'ien-i) would escape attention. How can she not be referred to as an extremely unfortunate person!

According to rumour, Miss Hŏ's poems are said to be all fake. For example, her lines, "When a wife is not the Spinning Damsel, how could the husband be the Herdboy," are also from a Chinese poem.

The fact is that these lines are not to be found in her collection. Since Yi Tŏngmu does not quote any other lines of her poems as being plagiarized his argument is flawed and can be disregarded.

Source 12.2   Extract from Yi Tŏngmu's *Ch'ŏngbirok*:[50]

"Okpong (Madam Yi, d. 1592?)[51] left thirty-two poems and eleven of them are included in *Lieh ch'ao shih chi*. Out of the eleven, poems with the titles like, "Complaint of Speckled Bamboo" (*Panjuk wŏn*) and "Lotus Gatherers" (*Ch'aeryŏn kok*) are included in Son'gok's (Yi Tal) collection. A line from "Autumn Plaint" (*Ch'uwŏn*) which reads:

Waking from a dream, I find the silk coverlet half empty.

is included in Nansŏrhŏn's collection."

However, this is erroneous, because it is not just one line, but all four lines of "Autumn Plaint" which are identical to those of Nansŏrhŏn's. Furthermore, the poem entitled, "Spring Day: Recollection" (*Ch'unil yuhoe*) by Nansŏrhŏn and that by Okpong are exactly the same. Okpong *shi*, which is included in *Karim sego purok* consists of thirty-two of Okpong's poems. These two poems, "Autumn Plaint" and "Spring Day: Recollection," a mere two out of thirty-two poems, are identical to Nansŏrhŏn's poems bearing the same titles. There is no evidence to support the originality of either poet's work, at this stage, in regard to these two poems.

---

50. Yi Tŏngmu, *op. cit.*, vol. 2, pp. 455-6.
51. Royal Secretary (承旨) Cho Wŏn's 趙瑗 (fl. 1572) concubine.

Source 13   Extract from Kim Shiyang's (1581-1643, styled Hadam)
                   Pugye kimun: [52]

"Nansŏrhŏn, a wife of Kim Sŏngnip and a sister of Hŏ Kyun possessed literary ability, but she died young. Her brother collected her work under the title of *Nansŏrhŏn chip*, with a preface by the envoy from China with lavish praise. Some people say that many of her poems are taken from the work of others. But I did not believe them until I was exiled to Chongsŏng and obtained a collection of Ming poetry. Upon consulting "Drums and Flutes amongst the People" I saw that eight characters out of one of the *yulsi* in her collection:

瑤裙振雪春雲暖
Green skirt shakes off the snow;
    warm spring clouds.
瓊佩鳴空夜月寒
A red stone pendant jingles in the sky;
    cold moon at night.[53]

are included in the poems "Drums to Flute," by a poet of the Yung-lo reign, Wu Shih-chung. Alas! I started to believe the statement made by some people who say that some of her poems are taken from the works of Chinese poets in the hope of deceiving Chinese eyes. This is no different from robbing someone and selling it back to the person robbed.

Source 14   Extract from Pak Chiwŏn's *Yŏrha ilgi*:[54]

"Nansŏrhŏn's, (Miss Hŏ) poetry is included in Ch'ien Ch'ien-i's *Lieh Ch'ao shih chi* and Chu Yi-tsun's *Ming shih tsung* under the name of Kyŏngbŏn, which is given as her name or pen-name. Earlier, when I wrote a preface for Yi Tŏngmu's *Ch'ŏngbirok*, I clarified this matter in detail. I heard that when Mugwan (Yi Tŏngmu) was in Yenching he showed her poetry to Academician (*Han-jen*) Chu Te-lin and Deputy Director (*Lang-chung*) T'ang Le-yu as well as (*She-jen*) P'an T'ing yun, all of whom read it in turn and admired it greatly. When I was in Yenching discussing gaps and mistakes in the anthology, I also talked about Miss Hŏ. Yin-kun then told me that, in his *Wai kuo chu chih tz'u*, the editor Yu T'ung (styled Hui-an) begins the first page of his anthology with a poem about your country. It reads:

---

52. Kim Shiyang, Pugye kimun. *TDYS, kwŏn* 72, vol. 13, p. 491. See also R. Rutt, *op. cit.*, p. 126.
53. The 5th and 6th lines of her poem entitled,"Escorting a Court Lady to the Taoist Temple (送宮人入道)," 7 syllable regulated verse. However, the lines Kim Shiyang quotes as taken from Wu Shih-chung's are different from Nansŏrhŏn's lines—five syllables out of fourteen are different. This is not good enough to support his argument and therefore, his basis for argument is not well-founded.
54. Pak Chiwŏn, *Yŏrha ilgi, op. cit.*, *kwŏn* 12, on T'aehak yugwannok 太學留館錄, p. 207.

> At Yanghwa Ford the red apricot blossoms;
> The folk-songs of eight provinces are
>   in the style of the Eastern Land.
> Fei-ch'iung, the Taoist nun, is thought about a great deal;
> She has already reached the Kuang-han Palace
>   to write on the ridge pole."

In his commentary Pak states that a literary woman, Hŏ Kyŏngbŏn, had later become a Taoist and that before doing so she wrote the prose entitled "Inscriptions on the Ridge Pole of the White Jade Tower in the Kwanghan Palace." I clarified the mistake about the name Kyŏngbŏn insofar as:

> "The name Kyŏngbŏn was taken out of respect for the Taoist Lady Fan and not in admiration of the handsome appearance of Fan-ch'uan (Tu Mu)."

Both Yin-kung and Ch'i-kung recorded this and each preserved his record. I am sure writers in China have something to say about the matter. Generally speaking, it is not proper for a lady to write poetry, but I cannot but admit that it is a great honour for a Korean to have her good reputation spread abroad. However, neither name nor pen-name of this lady of our land has even appeared within the country, so the record of just one pen- name, Nansŏrhŏn, should have been more than enough. Instead, they acknowledged Kyŏngbŏn as her name and recorded it here and there so that it is now impossible to rectify the mistake. This should be a warning to the female intellectuals of future generations that they must be very careful."

Another extract from *Yŏrha ilgi*: [55]

> "Hŏ Pong's younger sister, Miss Hŏ, has the pen-name Nansŏrhŏn. According to her biography she was a Taoist. In fact, there was no Taoist monastery or Taoist nun in our country. It also gives Kyŏngbŏn-dang as her pen-name which is a worse mistake than the other. Miss Hŏ married Kim Sŏngnip who had an odd appearance. His friends used to tease him saying that his wife worshipped Fan ch'uan. In general, it is not proper for a girl to write poetry. Furthermore, to spread the rumour around that she admired Tu Mu was really ridiculous."

Conclusion

These fourteen traditional sources (eleven Korean and Three Chinese) which relate to Nansŏrhŏn's poems have been translated and presented. Seven of the fourteen express conviction that plagiarism has taken place, not necessarily by the poetess herself, but by the hand of her brother, Hŏ Kyun, at the time of compilation of her collection. Of these seven sources, three are based on the findings of source number six. This reduces to four those sources which

---

55. *Ibid.*, *kwŏn* 14, on P'isŏrok 避暑錄, p. 275.

actually rely on their own findings. The four sources, with the exception of source number six, fail to provide tangible evidence sufficient to affirm that Nansŏrhŏn flagrantly plagiarised the poems of others to embellish her own work, rather than the imitation of poetic themes (as well as titles) and poetic language.

Source number 6 produces ten lines of complete plagiarism and four lines of combination, from the following parts of Nansŏrhŏn's work,

2 lines out of 87 poems of "Wandering Immortals";

1 line from "Song of the Willow Branches";

5 lines from 20 poems of "Palace Song" and another four lines of combination–said to be the combination of 2 lines from Chinese poetry of the same title;

2 lines of "Written to Rhyme Pattern of Sung of the Courtesan's Quarter's."

This is firm evidence that only a mere fourteen lines out of an impressive total work of two hundred and fourteen poems can be proved to have been plagiariazed from Chinese poems, not essentially by the author, but reputedly by her brother, Hŏ Kyun.

The authenticity, or otherwise, of Nansŏrhŏn's work, has to be considered, not only on the affirmative and negative sources provided herein, but by a full and unbiased assessment of the biographical record, historical material and the translations of her poetry. It appears to the writer that three substantial points must be made. Firstly, the poetic tradition of the period was to study the High T'ang poets and to imitate their best qualities, in order to bring Korean poetry to a state of perfection, by conforming with the (then) fashionable neo-Classical movement of the Ming dynasty's Seven Masters. Secondly, a majority of Nansŏrhŏn's poems are written in *akpu* style, which means that readers frequently find among her collection many titles which are either identical with, or bear a very close resemblance to, those of Chinese poems. This is because these poems are the reworking of themes drawn from the folk-song tradition of earlier times. This in itself has caused increasing doubt to be expressed as to the authenticity of her poems. Lastly, and most importantly, when reading through her complete work, one finds consistency in her treatment of poetic themes, both in the titles of her own creation and in those which were imitated. Nansŏrhŏn's poems are pervaded with an undeniable indigenous Korean femininity, a characteristic which Korean women readers, such as O Haein and Kim Yongsuk, who shared to some extent a common intuition, readily identified.

The accusation of plagiarism has been substantiated only in a very minor portion of Nansŏrhŏn's poems and even so, there is reason to believe that this occurred later, during the compilation of her work by her brother, Hŏ Kyun.

In the writer's opinion, this minute amount of plagiarism cannot be attributed to Nansŏrhŏn herself. Even though we must accept its existence, the fact remains that it is completely overshadowed by the importance of the three foregoing points which directly favour the authenticity of Nansŏrhŏn's poetry. Accordingly, the writer has no occasion other than to assert the authenticity of Nansŏrhŏn's poetry, subject to the minor reservation which this study of her work has revealed.

Bibliography

Books

Birrell, Anne. *New Songs from a Jade Terrace: An Anthology of Chinese Love Poetry*, London, Allen & Unwin, 1982.

Bielenstein, Hans. *The Bureaucracy of Han Times*, Cambridge, Cambridge University Press, 1980.

Ch'a Ch'ŏllŏ 車千輅. *Osan sŏllim ch'ogo* 五山說林草藁, *TDYS, kwŏn* 5, vol. 1, pp. 596-672.

Ch'a Chuhwan 車柱環. *Han'guk togyo sasang yŏn'gu* 韓國道敎思想硏究, Seoul, Sŏul Taehakkyo Ch'ulp'anbu, 1983.

_____. ed. *Shihwa wa mallok* 詩話와 漫錄, Seoul, 1966. (*Han'guk kojŏn munhak taegye* 韓國古典文學大系, vol. 19).

Chang Chin 張眞. "Hŏ Nansŏrhŏn non" 許蘭雪軒論, *Tongak ŏmun nonjip* 東岳語文論集, vol. 12, 1980.

Chang Kuang-p'i 張光弼. *Ssu k'u chüan shu chen pen ch'u chi* 四庫全書珍本初集.

Cheng Ch'iao 鄭樵. *T'ung chih* 通志, 10 vols., Taipei, T'ai-wan Chung-hua shu chü 1959.

Ch'ien Ch'ien-i 錢謙益. *Chiang yün lou shu mu* 絳雲樓書目, Peking, 1958.

_____. *Lieh Ch'ao shih chi* 列朝詩集, woodblock print, 25 vols, vol. 25.

Ch'iu Chun. *Ch'iu wen chuang kung ts'ung shu* 丘文莊公叢書, reproduction, Taipei, 1972, vol. 2.

Cho Tongil 趙東一. *Han'guk munhak sasangsa shiron* 韓國文學思想史試論, Seoul, Chishik Sanŏpsa, 1979.

_____. *Han'guk munhak t'ongsa* 韓國文學通史, 5 vols., Seoul, Chishik Sanŏpsa, 1989.

Chŏng Inji 鄭麟趾, ed. *Koryŏsa* 高麗史. Yŏnse Taehakkyo. Tongbanghak Yŏn'guso 東方學硏究所 ed. photo-reprint ed., 3 vols., Seoul, Asea Muhwasa, 1972.

Chōsen Sōtokufu 朝鮮總督府, ed., *Chōsen kinseki sōran* 朝鮮金石總覽, photo-reprint ed., 2 vols., Tokyo, Kokusho Kankōkai, 1971.

Chōsen Sŏtokufu 朝鮮總督府. *Chōsen tosho kaidai* 朝鮮圖書解題, photo-reprint ed., Tokyo, Nihon Tosho Senta, 1965.

Chu I-tsun 朱彝尊, ed. *Ming shih tsung* 明詩綜, 1705 ed., 3 vols.

Ch'u tz'u 楚辭. Chu Hsi 朱熹, ed., *Ch'u tz'u chi chu*, 6 vols., Peking, Jen min wen hsüeh ch'u pan she, 1953 ed.

Ch'u tz'u 楚辭. David Hawkes tr. *Ch'u tz'u* 楚辭: *The Songs of the South*, Oxford, 1959.

Ch'uan Han San kuo Chin Nan-pei ch'ao shih 全漢三國晋南北朝詩, Ting Fu-pao 丁福保 ed., 2 vols., Shanghai, 1959.

Ch'üan T'ang shih 全唐詩. Ts'ao Yin et. al., ed., 25 vols., Chung hua shu chü ed., Peking, 1960.

Chu-ko Yüan-sheng 諸葛元聲. *Liang ch'ao P'ing-jang lu* 兩朝平壤綠, photo-reprint ed., 5 vols., Taipei, 1969.

Covell, Alan Carter. *Ecstasy: Shamanism in Korea*, Seoul, Hollym International Corp., 1983.

Creel, Herrlee G. *What is Taoism? And Other Studies in Chinese Cultural History*, Chicago, University of Chicago Press, 1970.

Fei Ch'ang-fang 費長房. *Hou-Han shu* 後漢書.

Frankel, Hans H. *The Flowering Plum and the Palace Lady: Interpretations of Chinese Poetry*, New Haven, Yale University Press, 1976.

Frodsham, J.D. *An Anthology of Chinese Verse: Han Wei Chin and the Northern and Southern Dynasties*, Oxford, Clarendon Press, 1967.

_____. *The Poems of Li Ho* 李賀, Oxford, 1970.

Han Ch'iyun. *Haedong yaksa* 海東繹史, photo-reprint ed., 2 vols., Seoul, Kŏngin Munhwasa, 1974.

Hawkes, David. "The Quest of the Goddess." Cyril Birch. *Studies in Chinese Literary Genres*, Berkeley, 1974.

_____. *Ch'u Tz'u: The Song of the South*, Oxford, Clarendon Press, 1959.

Hiraoka Takeo 平岡武夫. *Tōdai no sijin*, 唐代の詩人, Kyōto, Kyōto Daigaku, 1960. (*Tōdai kenkyū no shiori*, 4)

_____. *Tōdai no sihen*, (Kyōto, Kyōto Daigaku Jimbun Kagaku Kenkyūjo 1964). (*Tōdai kenkyū no shiori*, 11-12).

Hŏ Kyun 許筠. *Haksan ch'odam* 鶴山樵談, *HKCS*, pp. 465-487.

_____. *Chang san'injŏn* 張山人傳 in *HKCS*, p. 105.

_____. *Changsaeng chŏn* 蔣生傳 in *HKCS*, pp. 110-111.

_____. *Hong Kiltong chŏn* 洪吉童傳 in *HKCS*, pp. 3-40 (2nd group).

_____. *Hŏ Kyun chŏnsŏ* 許筠全書. Yi I-hwa 李離和 ed. *Hŏ Kyun chŏnsŏ* 許筠全書, photo-reprint ed., Seoul, Asea Munhwasa, 1980.

_____. *Kukcho shisan* 國朝詩刪, Han'gukhak Munhŏn Yŏn'guso. 韓國學文獻研究所, ed. *Ch'ŏn'gu p'unga* 青丘風雅, *Kukcho shisan* 國朝詩刪, photo-reprint ed., Seoul, Asea Munhwasa, 1980.

_____. *Namgung sŏnsaeng chŏn* 南宮先生傳 in *HKCS*, pp. 105-110

_____. *Sŏngso pokpugo* 惺所覆瓿藁, *HKCS*, pp. 3-249.

_____. *Sŏngsu shihwa* 惺叟詩話 in *HKCS*, pp. 234-243.

Hŏ Nansŏrhŏn 許蘭雪軒. *Nansŏrhŏn chip*蘭雪軒集 (Title page: *Nansŏrche chip* 蘭雪齊集), Hŏ Kyun 許筠 ed. preface by Chu Chih-fan 朱之蕃. dated, 1606, reprint ed., of 1632 woodblock prints, 1692.

Holzman, Donald. *Poetry and Politics: The Life and Works of Juan Chi, AD 210-263*, Cambridge, Cambridge University Press, 1976.

Hong Manjong 洪萬宗. *Hong Manjong chŏnjip* 洪萬宗全集, photo-reprint ed., 2 vols., Seoul, T'aehaksa, 1980.

_____. *Shihwa ch'ongnim* 詩話叢林, photo-reprint ed., Seoul, Asea Munhwasa, 1973.

_____. *Sunoji* 旬五志. *Hong Manjong chŏnjip* 洪萬宗全集, vol. 1, pp. 1-122.

Hsiao T'ung 蕭統. *Wen hsüuan* 文選, (Peking, 1974 reprint), Peking, Chung hwa shu chü, 1974.

Hsü Ching 徐兢. *Kao li t'u ching* 高麗圖經, photo-reprint ed., Seoul, Asea Munhwasa, 1972.

Hsü Ling 徐陵. *Yü-t'ai hsin yung* 玉臺新詠, *Kuo hsüeh chi pen ts'ung shu* ed.

Hu Chen-heng 胡震亨. *T'ang-yin t'ung-kuei* 唐音統籤, Shanghai, Shang-hai ku chi ch'u pan she, 1981.

Hwang Hyŏn 黃玹. *Maech'ŏn shijip* 梅泉詩集, Pak Hyŏngdŏk ed., Seoul, 1932.

_____. *Maech'ŏn chip* 梅泉集, Kugyousa, 1980.

_____. *Tokkukcho chegashi* 讀國朝諸家詩 in *Maech'ŏn Shijip*, vol. 2.

Kang Hyosŏk 姜斅錫. *Chŏn'go taebang* 典故大方, photo-reprint ed., Seoul, Asea Munhwasa 1975.

Kim Pushik 金富軾. *Samguk Sagi* 三國史記, Yi Pyŏngdo 李丙燾, ed. 2 vols., Seoul, Ŭryu Munhwasa, 1977.

Kim Manjung 金萬重. *Sŏp'o chip* 西浦集, *Sŏp'o manp'il* 西浦漫筆, photo-reprint ed., Seoul, T'ongmun'gwan, 1971.

Kim Shisŭp 金時習. *Maewŏl-tang chip* 梅月堂集. Sejong Taewang Kinyŏm Saŏphoe 世宗大王記念事業會, *Kugyŏk Maeŏl-tang chip* 國譯梅月堂集, 3 vols., Seoul, 1982.

_____. *Kŭmo shinhwa* 金鰲新話.

Kim Yongsuk 金用淑. *Chosŏnjo yŏryu munhak ŭi yŏn'gu* 朝鮮朝 女流文學의 研究, Seoul, 1979.

_____. *Yijo ŭi yŏryu munhak* 李朝의女流 文學, Seoul, 1975. (*Ch'unch'u mun'go* 春秋文庫, 016).

Ko Hung 葛洪. *Pao-p'u tzu* 抱朴子, James Ware, tr. *Alchemy, Medicine, Religion in the China of A. D. 320: The Nei P'ien* 內篇 *of Ko Hung* 葛洪, Cambridge, Mass., The MIT Press, 1966.

_____. *Shen hsien chuan* 神仙傳, *Han-Wei ts'ung shu* 漢魏叢書, 1895 ed. Shanghai, 1896.

Kukcho pangmok 國朝榜目. photo-reprint ed., Seoul, Taehan Min'guk Kukhooe Tosŏgwan, 1971.

Kuo Mao-ch'ien 郭茂倩, ed. *Yüeh fu shih chi* 樂府詩集, *Chung-kuo ku tien wen hsüeh chi pen ts'ung shu*, Peking, Chung-hua shu chü, 1979.

Kuo P'u 郭璞, ed. *Mu T'ien-tzu chuan* 穆天子傳. *Ku chin i shih* ed., Shanghai, Shang wu yin shu kuan, 1937.

Kwŏn Kukchung. *Ch'amdonggye chuhae* 參同契註解.

Li Fang 李昉, ed. *Wen yüan ying hua* 文苑英華, Taipei, Hua wen shu chü, 1965.

_____. *T'ai p'ing kuang chi* 太平廣記, 4 vols., Shanghai, Ku chi chu pan she: Hsin hua shu tien Shang-hai fa hsing so fa hsing, 1990.

Li Ho 李賀. *Li Ch'ang-chi ko shih* 李長吉歌詩, Wang ch'i 王琦 ed., Taipei, Taiwan, Chung hua shu chü, 1965.

Li Hsien 李賢. *Huang-t'ai kua-tz'u* 黄臺苽辭.

Li Shang-yin 李商隱. *Li Yi-shan wen chi* 李義山文集, 5 vols.,Taipei, Taiwan shang wu yin shu kuan, 1967. *Ssu pu ts'ung k'an* ed.

Chao Shih-chieh and Chu Hsi-lun, ed. *Li tai nü tz'u shih chi* 歷代女子詩集, Taipei, Kuang wen shu chü yu hsien kung ssu, 1972.

Liu Hsiang 劉向. *Lieh hsien chuan* 列仙傳, *Chu tzu pai chia tsung shu*, Shanghai, Shanghai ku chi chu pan she, 1990.

_____. *Lieh nü chuan* 列女傳. *Ssu pu pei yao*. Shih pu, Taipei, Taiwan Chung hua shu chü, 1965.

Liu, James J. Y. *The Art of Chinese Poetry*, Chicago, University of Chicago Press, 1966.

_____. *The Poetry of Li Shang-yin* 李商隱, Chicago, University of Chicago Press, 1968.

Liu I-ch'ing 劉義慶. *Shih shuo hsin yu* 世說新語, Richard B. Mather, tr. *A New Account of the Tales of the World*, Minneapolis, University of Minnesota Press, 1976.

Liu, Ts'un-yan. *Buddhist and Taoist Influences on Chinese Novels*, Hong Kong, 1962.

_____. *Selected Papers From the Hall of Harmonious Wind*, Leiden, 1976.

Lü Ta-lin 呂大臨. *K'ao ku t'u* 考古圖, 6 vols. in 1 case, 1752.

Maeno Naoaki 前野直彬, *Tōshi kanshō jiten*, Tokyo, Tōkyōdō 1973.

_____. *Tōsisen* 唐詩選, Tokyo, Iwanami shoten, 1963.

Miao, Ronald, ed. *Studies in Chinese Poetry and Poetics*, San Francisco, Chinese Materials Centre, 1978.

Min Pyŏngdo 閔丙燾, ed. *Chosŏn yŏktae yŏryu munjip* 朝鮮歷代女流文集, Seoul, 1950.

Mun Kyŏnghyŏn 文暻鉉. "*Nansŏrhŏn yŏn'gu* 蘭雪軒研究," Kugŏ Kungmunhakhoe 國語國文學會, ed. *Hanmunhak Yŏn'gu* 漢文學研究, pp. 312-343, (*Kungmunhakhoe yŏn'gu ch'ongsŏ* 國文學會研究叢書, vol. 7), Seoul, Chŏngŭmsa, 1986.

_____. *Hŏ Nansŏrhŏn chŏnjip* 許蘭雪軒全集 Seoul, 1972.

Mu t'ien tzu chuan 穆天子傳. Cheng Te-k'un, tr. *The Travels of Emperor Mu*, *JNCBRAS*, 64, 1933, pp. 124-143.

Myŏngjong Taewang shillok 明宗大王實錄 in *CWS*.

Nansŏrhŏn chip 蘭雪軒集, Mun Kyŏnghyŏn tr. *Hŏ Nansŏrhŏn chŏnjip* 許蘭雪軒全集, Seoul, 1972.

Nansŏrhŏn chip 蘭雪軒集, O Haein 吳海仁, tr. *Nansŏrhŏn shijip* 蘭雪軒詩集, Seoul, Haein munhwasa, 1980.

Obata, Shigeyoshi. *The Works of Li Po*, Tokyo, 1935.

Owen, Stephen. *The Great Age of Chinese Poetry : The High T'ang*, New Haven, Yale University Press, 1981.

_____. *The Poetry of the Early T'ang*, New Haven, Yale University Press, 1977.

Pak Chiwŏn 朴趾源. *Yŏnam chip* 燕巖集, photo-reprint ed., Seoul, Kŏnghŭi Ch'ulp'ansa, 1966.

_____. *Yŏrha ilgi* 熱河日記, *Han'guk Myŏngjŏ Taejŏnjip: Yŏnam hanmun sosŏl*, Seoul, Taeyang Sojŏk, 1984.

Pan Ku 班固. *Han Wu- ti nei chuan* 漢武帝內傳, *Han Wei ts'ung shu*, 1895 ed.

_____. *Han shu* 漢書, Chung hua shu chü 中華書局 ed., Peking, Hsin hua shu tien, 1962.

P'eng Kuo-tung 彭國棟. *Chung-Han shih shi* 中韓詩史. Shin Hoyŏl 辛鎬烈 tr., Han-Chung shisa 韓中詩史, 2 vols., Seoul, Republic of Korea. Kongboshil, 1960.

Rutt, Richard. *The Bamboo Grove: An Introduction to Shijo*, Berkeley, University of California Press, 1971.

Sailey, Jay. *The Master Who Embraces Simplicity: A Study of the Philosopher Ko Hung* 葛洪, *283-343*, San Francisco, Chinese Materials Centre, 1978.

Shih chi 史記. Chung-hua shu-chü ed.

_____. *Feng shan shu* 封禪書, *chüan* 28.

Shih ching 詩經.

Shin Hum 申欽. *Ch'ŏng ch'ang yŏndam* 晴窓軟談, Hong Manjong 洪萬宗. *Shihwa ch'ongnim* 詩話叢林, pp. 219-233.

Sung shih 宋史. Chung hua shu chü ed.

Taedong yasŭng 大東野乘. photo-reprint of 1909 ed., published by Chŏsŏn Kŏjŏn Kanhaenghoe 朝鮮古典刊行會, 13 vols., Seoul, 1968.

T'ao Hung-ching. *Ling pao chen ling wei yeh t'u, Ts'ung shu chi ch'eng* 叢書集成 (1st series) ed.

Tung-fang Shuo 東方朔 (Attributed to). *Hai nei shih chou chi* 海內十州記, *Ku-chin i shih* ed.

_____. *Han Wu-ti ku shih* 漢武帝故事, *Han-Wei ts'ung shu*, 1895 ed.

_____. *Shih chou chi* 十州記, *Ku-shin i-shih* ed.

_____. *Tung-fang Shuo chuan* 東方朔傳 in *Han Shu chüan* 65.

Vervoorn, Aat. *A Man of the Cliffs and Caves*, Hong Kong, Chinese University Press, 1990.

Wang Chia 王嘉. *Shih i chi* 拾遺記, *Ku-chin i-shi* 古今逸史 ed.

_____. *P'eng-lai (Shan)* 蓬萊山 in *Shih i chi*, *chüan* 10.

Wang Kuei 王珪. *Hua yang chi* 華陽集, *Tsung shu chi ch'eng* 叢書集成 no. 1912.

Watson, Burton. *Chinese Lyricism*, New York, Colombia University Press, 1971.

_____. *Chinese Rhyme Prose*, New York, Columbia University Press, 1971.

_____. *Early Chinese Literature*, New York, Columbia University Press, 1962.

_____. *Su Tung-p'o* 蘇東坡, New York, 1965.

Wei Hung. *Han kuan chiu i* 漢官舊儀, *Ts'ung shu chi ch'eng* 叢書集成 (1st series), Shanghai, 1935-1937. (no. 8111).

Werner. E.T.C. *A Dictionary of Chinese Mythology*, New York, The Julian Press, 1961.

Wu Ming-chi 吳明濟. *Ch'ao hsien shih hsüan* 朝鮮詩選.

Yang Hsiung 楊雄. *Shan hai ching* 山海經, Kuo P'u 郭璞, ed. *Ku chin i shih*, ed.

_____. *T'ai hsüan ching* 太玄經.

Yi Kŭngik 李肯翊, ed. *Yŏllyŏshil kisul* 燃藜室記述, Minjok Munhwa Ch'ujinhoe, ed. *Kugyŏk yŏllyŏshil kisul* 國譯燃藜室記述, 12 vols., Seoul, 1966-68.

Yi Kyugyŏng 李圭景. *Oju yŏnmun changjŏn san'go* 五洲衍文長箋稿, photo-reprint of Kojŏn Kanhaenghoe ed., 2 vols., Seoul, Tongguk Munhwasa, 1959.

Yi Nŭnghwa 李能和. *Chosŏn musokko* 朝鮮巫俗考, Yi Chaegon tr., Seoul, Paengnok Ch'ulp'ansa, 1976.

_____. *Chosŏn togyosa* 朝鮮道敎史, Yi Chongŭn tr., Seoul, Posŏng Munhwasa, 1981.

_____. *Chosŏn yŏsokko* 朝鮮女俗考, photo-reprint ed., Seoul, Taeyang Sŏjŏk, 1973, (*Han'guk myŏngjŏ taejŏnjip* 韓國名著大全集).

Yi Sugwang 李晬光. *Chibong yusŏl* 芝峰類說, photo-reprint ed., Seoul, Kyŏngin Munhwasa, 1970.

Yi Tŏngmu 李德懋. *Ch'ŏngjanggwan chŏnsŏ* 青莊館全書. Sŏul Taehakkyo Kŏjŏn Kanhaenghoe, ed. *Ch'ŏngjanggwan chŏnsŏ* 青莊館全書. photo-reprint ed., 3 vols., Seoul, 1966.

_____. *Ch'ŏngbirok* 青脾錄 in *Ch'ŏngjanggwan Chŏnsŏ, kwŏn* 32-39.

Yijo shillok 李朝實錄. Kuksa P'yŏnch'an Wiwŏnhoe 國史編纂委員會, ed. *Chosŏn wangjo shillok* 朝鮮王朝實錄, 48 vols., Seoul, 1955-1958.

Yu Sŏngnyong 柳成龍. *Sŏae munjip* 西厓文集, facsimile reproduction, Seoul, Sŏnggyun'gwan Taehakkyo 成均館大學校. Taedong Munhwa Yŏn'guwŏn, 1958.

Yun Kukhyŏng 尹國馨. *Munso mannok* 聞韶漫錄, *TDYS*, *kwŏn* 55, vol.10.

Articles

Ch'a Sang-ch'an 車相璨. "Hŏ Nansŏrhŏn 許蘭雪軒," *Pando sahwa wa nakt'o Manju* 半島史話와 樂土滿洲, 1942.

Chang Chugŭn 張籌根. "Han'guk ŭi musok," *Han'guk ŭi musok munhwa* 韓國의 巫俗文化, Seoul, Kukche Munhwa Chaedan, 1974.

Ch'oe Yongjin. "Yijo yŏryu chakp'um soron 李朝女流作品小論," Ihwa Taehakkyo, *Kugŏ kungmunhak yŏn'gu* 國語國文學研究, no. 1, 1958, pp. 82-94.

Cho Tong'il 趙東一. "The Study of Korean Literature as It Stands Now," *Korea Journal*, vol. 12, no. 9, 1981, p. 13.

Chŏn Kyut'ae 全圭泰. "Han-Chung shiga ŭi pigyo munhaktchŏk koch'al 韓中詩歌의 比較文學的考察," *Hyŏndae munhak* 現代文學, no. 315, 1981, pp. 290-318.

Downer, G.B. and Graham, A.C. "Tone Patterns in Chinese Poetry," London University School of Oriental and African Studies, *Bulletin*, vol. 26, 1963, pp. 145-48.

Funazu Tomihiko 船津富彦. "Kaku Haku no yūsensi no tokushitsu ni tsuite," *Tokyo Shina gakuhō*, no. 10, pp. 53-69.

_____. "Gi no Butei no Yūsen bungaku ni tsuite," Yoshioka Yoshitoyo Hakushi Kanreki Kinen Ronshū Kankōkai, ed. *Yoshioka hakushi kanreki kinen Dōkyōkenkyū ronshū* Tokyo, 1977, pp. 165-192.

_____. "Sō Shoku no yūsen siron," *Tōyōbungaku kenkyū*, no. 13, pp. 49-65.

_____. "Daijin-fu Siron," *Kan-Gi bunka*, no. 4, 1965, pp. 21-37.

Hŏ Mija. "Hŏ Ch'ohŭi ŭi yusŏnsa e nat'anan imiji yŏn'gu 許楚姬의 游仙詞에 나타난 이미지 研究," Tan'guk Taehakkyo. Taehagwŏn, ed. *Haksul nonch'ong* 學術論叢, no. 2, 1978, pp. 13-34.

Kim Kapki. "Nansŏrhŏn ŭi munhak kwa insaeng 蘭雪軒의 文學과 人生," Tongguk Taehakkyo. *Taehagwŏn yŏn'gu nonmunjip*, no. 7, 1977, p. 69.

Kim Tonguk. "Han'guk ŭi kyusu shiin Hŏ Nansŏrhŏn," Han'guk Immul Taegye P'yŏnch'an Wiwŏnhoe, ed. *Han'guk immul Taegye*, Seoul, 1972, vol. 4, *Yijo ŭi immul*, pt. 2.

_____. "Hwang Chini wa Hŏ Nansŏrhŏn," *Hyŏndae munhak*, vol. 1, no. 9, 1955, pp. 126-134.

Pak Yŏngu 朴英雨. "Chun'guk e sogae toen Hŏ kyun kwa Nansŏrhŏn 中國에 紹介된 許筠과 蘭雪軒," Ch'ŏn'gu Taehakkyo, ed. *Kugŏ kungmunhak yŏn'gu* 國語國文學研究, no. 1.

Pak Yosun. "Hŏ Nansŏrhŏn kwa kyuwŏn kago許蘭雪軒과 閨怨歌考," *Honam munhwa yŏn'gu* 湖南文化研究, no. 2, 1964, pp. 85-104.

Rutt, Richard. "Hanmun-Korean Literature in Chinese," *Korea Journal*, vol. 13, no. 3, pp. 4-8, Seoul, 1973.

_____. "Traditional Korean Poetry," *Transaction* XLVII, 1972, Seoul Royal Asiatic Society, Korea Branch, pp. 105-144.

Yang Yŏmgyu. "Hŏ Nansŏrhŏn kwa kŭŭi kasa," Tongguk Taehakkyo, *Kugŏ kungmunhak nonmunjip* 國語國文學論文集, no. 3, 1962, pp. 43-51.

Yi Usŏng 李佑成. "Koryŏ mal Yijo ch'ogi ŭi ŏbuga 高麗末李朝初期의 漁夫歌," *Sŏnggyun'gwan Taehakkyo nommunjip* 成筠館大學校論文集, vol. 9, 1964.

Index

An-ch'i (An ch'i Sheng) 安期生, 15, 75
Andong 安東, 11
Andong Kim 安東金氏, 10, 11
Angnok 岳麓, see Hŏ Sŏng
Ch'a Sangch'an 車相璨, 96, 38
Chaha 紫霞, see Shin Wi
Chami 紫微, 82
Chang Chin 張眞, 32
Chang Chugŭn 張籌根, 27
Chang Hu 張祜, 64
Chang Kuang-p'i, see Chang Yu
Chang Kuo-wei 張國維, 107
Chang Yu 張昰, 109
Chang-huai, Crown Prince 章懷太子, 51
Ch'ang-kan 長干, 45, 69, 70
Ch'ang-kan chü (Changgankok) 長干曲, 70
Ch'ang-men fu 長門賦, 81
Chao Fei-yen 趙飛燕, 80
Ch'en, Empress 陳(武后), 81
Chen chün 眞君, 34
Chen jen (chinin) 眞人, 34
Ch'en Tzŭ-ang 陣子昂, 49
Ch'eng, Emperor 成帝, 80
Ch'i ch'u ch'ang (Kich'ul ch'ang) 氣出昌, 85
Ch'i-kuo, Lord 岐國公, see Wang Kuei
Chiangnan-ch'ü (Kangnam kok) 江南曲, 73
Chibong 芝峰, see Yi Sugwang
Ch'ien Ch'ien-i 錢謙益, 31, 107-109,
    111-112, 114-115
Ch'ien Mu-chai 錢牧齊, 111
Chien-an 建安, 37, 98
Chien-ch'i tea 建溪茶, 79
Chien-wen, Emperor 簡文, 100
Ch'ih ching tzü (Chŏkchŏng-ja) 赤精子, 34
Ch'ih lung (Chŏgyong) 赤龍, 34
Chin 晋, 5, 33
Ch'in 秦, 2, 7, 15, 75
Chin ling 金陵, 112
Chin ling sheng mu 金靈聖母, 95
chin-t'i shih (kŭnch'e shi) 近體詩, 22
Ch'ing p'ing t'iao 清平調, 90
Ching-lieh (Chŏngnyŏl) 精列, 85
ch'ing-t'an (ch'ŏngdam) 清談, 25
Chinhŭng, King 眞興王, 21
chinsa 進士, 2, 28
Chiu ko 九歌, 37, 58
Chiu-i, Mountain (Kuŭi) 九疑山, 36

Cho Wŏn 趙瑗, 114
Ch'odang 草堂, 6, 8, 107, 113
Ch'oe Ch'iwŏn 崔致遠, 21
Chŏng Hŭiryang 鄭希良, 23-24
Chŏngja 正字, 110
ch'ŏnmin 賤民, 23
Chosŏn 朝鮮, 1, 5, 9-10, 17-18, 21-23, 25,
    27, 33, 38, 41, 78, 82, 103-104, 107
Ch'owŏl 草月, 11, 50
Chu Chih-fan 朱之蕃, 112
Chu Hsi 朱熹, 17
Chu Te-lin 祝德麟, 115
Ch'u tz'u 楚辭, 3, 36-37, 40, 96
Chu Yi-tsun 朱彝傳, 31, 105, 112, 115
chu-chih 竹枝, 37
Chu-ko Yüan-sheng 諸葛元聲, 31
Chuang tzu (Changja) 莊子, 18, 25
Chuang-yüan 狀元, 112
chüeh-chu (chŏlgu) 絶句, 64
Ch'un-ch'iu 春秋, 37
Chung-mo 仲默, see Ho Ching-Ming
Chungjong, King 中宗, 17, 19, 24, 28, 35
Ch'unil yuhoe 春日有懷, 114
Eastern Chin 東晉, 85
Eastern King 東皇, 88
Fan, Lady 樊夫人, 5, 11, 116
Fan-ch'uan 樊川, see Tu Mu
Fang, Madam 方夫人, 109
Fang Chang (Pangjang) 方丈, 34
Fang-hu (Pangho) 方壺, 34
Fei Ch'ang-fang 費長房, 35
Feng shen yen i 封神演義 in *Han Wu-ti nei
    chuan*, 34, 95
Feng-lin 鳳麟, 94
Fu ku (Pokko) 復古, 2
Fu sang (Pusang) 扶桑, 95
Hadam 荷潭, see Kim Shiyang
Haedong 海東, 7, 111
Hagok 荷谷, see Hŏ Pong
Hai-chung San Shan (Haejung Samsan) 海
    中三山, 35
Haksan 鶴山, see Hŏ Kyun
Han 漢, 2, 7, 15, 39, 46-48, 64, 73, 75, 80-
    81, 84, 87, 94, 100
Han shu 漢書, 36, 46, 80-81
Han-jen 翰人, 115
hanmun 漢文, 1, 2, 4, 27

hanshi 漢詩, 1, 3, 17, 32, 41, 66, 96
Ho Ching-ming 何景明, 28, 107
Hŏ Ch'odang 許草堂, see Hŏ Yŏp
Hŏ Ch'ohŭi 許楚姬, see Hŏ Nansŏrhŏn
Hŏ Kyŏngnan 許景蘭, 32
Hŏ Kyun 許筠, 3, 5-12, 14-15, 20-22, 24,
    26, 30-33, 51, 53, 75, 96-97, 102-106,
    108-109, 111, 113, 115-117
Hŏ Misuk 許美叔, see Hŏ Pong
Hŏ Nansŏrhŏn 許蘭雪軒, 1, 3, 5, 11, 32, 38,
    96, 105
Hŏ Pong 許篈, 2, 6, 15, 54, 103, 106, 111, 116
Hŏ Sŏng 許筬, 6
Ho Yen 何晏, 25
Hŏ Yŏp 許曄, 6, 10, 113
Hŏ Yŏp shindobi 許曄神道碑, 5
Ho-dang (Tongho Toksŏ-dang) 湖堂, 98
Hogok shihwa 壺谷詩話, 105-106
Hong Manjong 洪萬宗, 23, 26, 33, 106, 113
Hong Taeyong 洪大容, 103-104, 113-114
Hongmun'gwan chŏjak 弘文館著作, 12
Hsi Shan ching 西山經 in *Shan Hai Ching*,
    chüan 2., 86
Hsi wang mu (Sŏwangmo) 西王母, 86-87, 95
Hsi-ch'u ko (Sŏgok ka) 西曲歌, 64
Hsi-kung 西宮, 81
Hsiang, River 湘江, 36-37, 45, 55, 57
Hsiang chün (Sang gun) 湘君, 58
Hsiang fu jen (Sang puin) 湘夫人, 58
Hsiang-ho ko tz'u 相和歌辭, 42, 73
Hsiao Ch'ang-kan ch'ü (So Changgan kok)
    小長干曲, 70
Hsieh Tao-yün 謝道韞, 112
Hsieh T'iao 謝朓, 91
hsien (sŏn) 仙, 2, 3, 23-27, 29, 96, 109
Hsien T'ung 仙童, 88
Hsien-chi 獻吉, see Li Meng-Yang
Hsien-jen shih-chih (Hyŏnin silchi) 賢人失
    志, 49
Hsü (Hŏ) 虛, 75
Hsü Ling 徐陵, 91
Hsüan shih 亘史, 106
Hsüan tu (Hyŏndo) 玄都, 34
Hsüan-ho 宣和, 25
hsüan-hsüeh (hyŏnhak) 玄學, 25, 85
Hsüan-tsung, Emperor 玄宗, 90
Hsüan-tu Tung (Hyŏndo Dong) 玄都洞, 34
Hu lu 壺蘆, 94
Hu-weng 壺翁, 35
Hua, Mountain 華山, 38
Huang t'ai kua-tz'u 黃臺瓜辭, 51
Huang T'ing-chien 黃庭堅, 20
Hui-an 悔菴, see Yu T'ung
Hun'gu School 勳舊派, 17
Hupei 湖北, 69, 111
Hwang Hyŏn 黃玹, 9, 105, 107

hwarang-do 花郎道, 21
Hyo Ts'ui Kuo-fu ch'e 效崔國輔體, 42
Ijo 吏曹, 6
Imjin Waeran 壬辰倭亂, 7, 11, 108
In (Lin) 麟, 46
Inmok, Queen Mother 仁穆大妃, 9
Juan Chao 阮肇, 39
Juan Chi 阮籍, 49, 53
kan-yü (Kamu) 感遇, 49
Kangnam ak 江南樂, 73
Kangnam su 江南愁, 73
Kao-tsung, Emperor 高宗, 51
Kapcha Sahwa 甲子士禍, 19, 27
Kapsan 甲山, 7, 54, 103
kasa 歌辭, 1, 32-33, 42, 75
Kim Chin 金振, 11
Kim Hyowŏn 金孝元, 7
Kim Manjung 金萬重, 11, 111
Kim Pushik 金富軾, 21
Kim Shisŭp 金時習, 23-24, 26
Kim Shiyang 金時讓, 115
Kim Sŏngnip 金誠立, 10-12, 103, 106, 108,
    110, 112-113, 115-116
Kim Tujong 金斗鍾, 31
Kim Yongsuk 金用淑, 41, 117
kisaeng 妓生, 5, 8, 66
Ko Hung 葛洪, 15, 25, 86
Ko-p'o 葛陂, 35, 48
kobu 古賦, 32
Kojŏn Kanhaenghoe 古典刊行會, 25, 26
komun 古文, 7
Koryŏ 高麗, 2, 17, 33
Ku (Kuei) 龜, 46
ku-shih (koshi) 古詩, 22, 40
ku-tz'u (kosa) 古辭, 70
Kuang-chin 廣津, see Wang Yai
Kujung (chiu-ch'ung) 九重, 81
Kung yang chuan 公羊傳, 81
Kŭmo, Mt 金鰲山, 24
K'un-lun Shan (Kongnyun-san) 崑崙山, 87
kung-sa 宮詞, 79-84, 108-109
kung-t'i shih (Kungch'e shi) 宮體詩, 82
Kuo Mao-ch'ien 郭茂倩, 47
Kuo P'u 郭璞, 15, 85-87
Kwangnŭng 廣陵, 13, 50
Kwanghan Palace 廣寒殿, 8, 13, 102, 108,
    111-112, 116
Kwangju 廣州, 11, 50
Kwangsang, Mountain 廣桑山, 45, 94
Kyŏngan-ch'ŏn River 京安川, 50
Kyŏngbŏn 景樊, see Hŏ Nansŏrhŏn
Kyŏnggi 京畿, 6, 11, 50
Kyŏngsu (or Kyŏngshi) 鏡水, 11, 50
Kyosan 蛟山, see Hŏ Kyun
Lan-kung 蘭公, 113-114
Lan-yü 蘭嶼, see Chu Chih-fan

Lang-chung 郎中, 115
Lao Tzu (Noja) 老子, 18, 34
Later Han 後漢, 25, 39, 98
Li Chih 禮志 in *Sung Shih*, chap.105, 34
Li Ho 李賀, 14, 34, 35-36, 51, 73, 87
Li Hsien 李賢, 51
Li Meng-yang 李夢陽, 28, 107
Li P'an-lung 李攀龍, 107
Li Po 李白, 2, 7-8, 14, 35-36, 54, 63, 69-70, 72, 89-90, 95-96
Li sao (Iso) 離騷, 85
Li Shang-yin 李商隱, 34-36, 51, 73, 87
Liang 梁, 73, 100
Liang Yu-nien 梁有季, 30, 31
Liu Ch'e 劉徹, 87
Liu Hsiang 劉向, 86
Liu Ju-shih 柳如是, 108, 114
Liu Kang 劉綱, 5
Liu lang 劉郎, 87
Liu Yü-hsi 劉禹錫, 95
Lu Chi 陸機, 33
Lü shih (yulshi) 律詩, 22
lu yü chang (nogokchang) 綠玉杖, 35
Ma Hung 馬洪, see Ma Hao-lan
Ma Hao-lan 馬浩瀾, 109
Maech'ŏn 梅泉, see Hwang Hyŏn
Masuda Kiyohide 增田清秀, 42
Meng yu T'ien-mu yin 夢遊天姥吟, 95
Ming 明, 28, 31-32, 51, 109-112, 115, 117
Ming shih chi shih 明詩紀事, 107
Ming-kuang Palace 明光宮, 46
Mo-ch'ou 莫愁, 63-64
Mo-ch'ou ch'ü (Maksu kok) 莫愁曲, 63
Mo-ch'ou yüeh (Maksu ak) 莫愁樂, 63-64
Mu, King 穆王, 86-87, 95
Mu Wang (Mok wang) 穆王, 87
Mu-chai 牧齊, see Chien Chien-i
Mugwan 懋官, see Yi Tŏngmu
Mun Kyŏnghyŏn 文暻鉉, 10
Muo Sahwa 戊午士禍, 19, 27
Muok 巫玉, 33
musok 巫俗, 26
Nanking 南京, 69
Nam Yongik 南龍翼, 105-106
Nangnang 鸞郎, 21
Nangsŏn 浪仙, see Ŏ Mujŏk
Nansŏrhŏn 蘭雪軒, 1-3, 5-12, 14-15, 24, 26-27, 30-33, 35-44, 47, 49-51, 53, 61, 64, 66, 68-70, 72-73, 75-77, 83-85, 96-98, 100, 102-118
Noŭn-so 老隱沼, 50
Nŭnghŏsa 凌虛詞, 26
O Haein 吳海仁, 32, 66, 78, 117
Ŏ Mujŏk 魚無迹, 23-24
Ŏgao 魚家傲, 32

Okdang 玉堂, 106
Okpong 玉峯, 111, 114
pa ping 八病, 22
Pa-shui (P'asu) 巴水, 69
Paek Kwanghun 白光勳, 20, 53, 111
Paekpin 白蘋, 72
Pak Chiwŏn 朴趾源, 11, 105, 112, 115
Pak Sun 朴淳, 20, 22, 28
Pak Yŏngu 朴英雨, 31
Pan (Pan Chieh-yü), Lady 班婕妤, 80, 84, 112
Pan Ku 班固, 86
P'an-t'ao Hui 蟠桃會, 15, 87
panch'ŏng 半清, 100
Panjuk wŏn 斑竹怨, 114
pant'ak 半濁, 14
P'ei Shuo 裴說, 108
P'eng Kuo-tung 彭國棟, 105, 107
P'eng-hu (Pongho) 蓬壺, 34
Pi-hai (Pyŏkhae) 碧海, 95
pin 嬪, 82
Pinnyŏ ŭm 貧女吟, 42
Po-shan lu (Paksan no) 博山爐, 59
Pohŏsa 步虛詩, 26
Pongnae, Mountain 蓬萊山, 35, 48
Pongsŏnhwa ka 鳳仙花歌, 32
Pu ch'u hsia men hsing (poch'ul hamunhaeng) 步出夏門行, 85
Pu hsu tz'u (Pohŏsa) 步虛詩, 15
Pyŏngjo 兵曹, 6
P'yŏngyang 平攘, 31
sa 辭, 14, 32-33, 61, 75, 82-83, 85-86
Saganwŏn taesagan 司諫院大司諫, 6
Sajang School 詞章派, 17-19, 28
Sallim School 山林派, 17-20, 22, 23, 28
Sam-Tang shiin 三唐詩人, 2
Samshin, Mt 三神山, 25
Sangch'on 象村, 113
Sarim School 士林派, 17
She-jen 舍人, 115
Shen Yüeh 沈約, 73
Sheng-T'ang 盛唐, 2
Shih ching 詩經, 8, 16, 52, 64
Shih-ch'eng yüeh (Sŏksŏng-ak) 石城樂, 64
Shih-hsing 士行, see T'ao K'an
Shihŭng 始興, 6
shihwa 詩話, 26
shijo 時調, 1
Shilla 新羅, 8, 21, 27
Shim Ŭigyŏm 沈義謙, 7
Shin Hŭm 申欽, 105, 113
Shin Wi 申緯, 102
Shindong-myŏn (Township) 新東面, 6
Shui fu (Subu) 水府, 37
Shun, Emperor 舜帝, 36, 38, 53, 55

Shin Hoyŏl 辛鎬烈, 107
Sŏae 西厓, see Yu Sŏngnyong
Sŏin 西人, 7
Sŏnggyun'gwan Taesasŏng 成均館大司成, 6
Sŏngni 性理, 18
Son'gok 蓀谷, see Yi Tal
Sŏnjo, King 宣祖, 1, 9, 20, 24, 26, 28, 32,
  35, 96
Sŏnp'ung 仙風, 24
sŏŏl 庶蘗, 23
Sŏp'o 西浦, see Kim Manjung
Sŏp'yŏng, Prince 西平, 6
soŭi 昭儀, 82
sowŏn 昭媛, 82
Soyong 昭容, 82
Ssu-ma Hsiang-ju 司馬相如, 81
Su Shih 蘇軾, 20
Su Tung-p'o 蘇東坡, see Su Shih
sugŭi 淑儀, 82
Sui 隋, 75
Sung 宋, 2, 17, 20, 25, 28, 47, 109, 113, 117
Sung, Mount 嵩山, 15, 38
Ta-lo (Taera) Palace 大羅宮, 34
Tamhŏn 湛軒, see Hong Taeyong
T'ang Chen 唐震, 111
Tanhak 丹學, 24
T'ao, Lord 陶公, 111
T'ao K'an 陶侃, 111
T'ien-mu, Mountain 天母山, 95-96
Tojangnyu 道藏類 in Oju yŏnmun changjŏn
  san'go, kwŏn, 26
Tongin 東人, 7
Tongnae magistracy 東萊府, 31
Tou-mu 斗母, 95
Toyotomi Hideyoshi 豊臣秀吉, 7
Ts'a-ch'ü ko tz'ü (chapkok kasa) 雜曲歌辭,
  75
Ts'ai lien ch'ü (Ch'aeryŏn kok) 采蓮曲, 100
Ts'an t'ung ch'i (Ch'amdonggye) 參同契,
  38, 53
Ts'ang-wu, Mountain 蒼梧山, 36-38, 57
Ts'ao Chih 曹植, 33
Ts'ao T'ang 曹唐, 15, 108, 111
Ts'eng-chi 曾稽, 31, 109
Ts'ui Hao 崔顥, 70
Ts'ui Kuo-fu 崔國輔, 42, 45, 67-68
Ts'ung shu chi ch'eng 叢書集成, 80, 109
Tu Fu 杜甫, 2, 8, 20, 107
Tu kong pu (chip) 杜工部(集), 8, 20, 107
Tu Mu 杜牧, 11, 103, 113, 116
T'ung ch'eng 桐城, 109
Tung Wang-kung (Tong Wang-gong) 東王
  公, 88
Tung-fang Shuo 東方朔, 81, 86, 94

tz'u (sa) 辭, 14, 64, 115
Tzu-wei hsing (Chami sŏng) 紫微星, 82
Tzu-yün 子雲, see Yang Hsiung
Wan-li 萬歷, 31, 107
Wang Chi chüan 王吉傳 in Han Shu,
  Chüan 72
Wang Chia 王嘉, 34-35, 88
Wang Chien, 王建, 109
Wang Chung-ch'u, 王仲初, see Wang Chien
Wang Kuei 王珪, 109
Wang Pi 王弼, 25
Wang Shih-chen 王世貞, 28, 107
Wang Wei 王維, 2
Wang Yai 王涯, 108
Wei 魏, 15, 33, 47, 73, 85-86
Wei Hung 衛宏, 80
Wen T'ing-yun 溫庭筠, 73
Wu, Emperor 武帝, 15, 46, 75, 81, 85-87,
  93-94
Wu ch'ang 武昌, 111-112
Wu chung 吳中, 109
Wu Ming-chi 吳明濟, 31, 109
Wu Shih-chung 吳世忠, 115
Wu Tzu-yu, see Wu Ming-chi
Wu Yü (Oak) 五嶽, 100
Yang, Emperor 煬帝, 75
Yang Hsiung 揚雄, 47
Yang Kuei-fei, Lady 楊貴妃, 90
Yang-chou 揚州, 69
yangban 兩班, 31, 8, 24, 33, 66
Yangch'ŏn 陽川, 6
Yangtze, River 楊子江, 37, 55, 62, 69, 71-
  73, 91, 100-101
Yangyuji sa 楊柳枝詞, 43
Yao, Emperor 堯帝, 55
Yejo 禮曹, 6
Yi Kyugyŏng 李圭景, 26
Yi Sugwang 李睟光, 20-22, 32, 98-100,
  105, 110-111
Yi Tal 李達, 2, 7-8, 20, 22, 35, 111-112,
  114
Yi Tŏngmu 李德懋, 113
Yi Usŏng 李佑成, 18
Ying 瀛, 94
Ying-chou (Yŏngju) 瀛州, 34
Ying-hu (Yŏngho) 瀛壺, 34
Yoji 搖池, 87
Yong (Lung) 龍, 46
Yongin 龍仁, 6
Yu hsien shih (Yusŏnsa) 遊仙詞, 85-90
Yü Ju-chou 俞汝舟, 66
Yü Nü 玉女, 88
Yu Sŏngnyong 柳成龍, 15-16, 106
Yü Shun, Emperor Shun 虞舜, 38

Yu ssu shih hua 玉篦詩話, 107
Yu T'ung 尤侗, 115
Yu-hsieh (Yuhyŏp, "bravo") 遊俠, 21, 47
Yüan 元, 25, 94, 109, 111-112
Yüan-shih 怨詩, 68
Yüeh 越, 80
yüeh-fu (akpu) 樂府, 3, 21-22, 33, 41-43,
    64, 68, 83, 98-99, 111
yulshi 律詩, 22, 32, 41, 84
Yun Kukhyŏng 尹國馨, 7
Yung-huai 詠懷, 49, 53
Yusŏnsa 遊仙詞, 26, 37-39

CORNELL EAST ASIA SERIES

4 Fredrick Teiwes, *Provincial Leadership in China: The Cultural Revolution and Its Aftermath*

8 Cornelius C. Kubler, *Vocabulary and Notes to Ba Jin's* Jia: *An Aid for Reading the Novel*

16 Monica Bethe & Karen Brazell, *Nō as Performance: An Analysis of the Kuse Scene of* Yamamba

17 Royall Tyler, tr., *Pining Wind: A Cycle of Nō Plays*

18 Royall Tyler, tr., *Granny Mountains: A Second Cycle of Nō Plays*

23 Knight Biggerstaff, *Nanking Letters, 1949*

28 Diane E. Perushek, ed., *The Griffis Collection of Japanese Books: An Annotated Bibliography*

36 Miwa Kai, tr., edited & annotated by Robert J. Smith & Kazuko Smith, *The Diary of a Japanese Innkeeper's Daughter*

37 J. Victor Koschmann, Ōiwa Keibō & Yamashita Shinji, eds., *International Perspectives on Yanagita Kunio and Japanese Folklore Studies*

38 James O'Brien, tr., *Murō Saisei: Three Works*

40 Kubo Sakae, *Land of Volcanic Ash: A Play in Two Parts,* revised edition, tr. David G. Goodman

44 Susan Orpett Long, *Family Change and the Life Course in Japan*

48 Helen Craig McCullough, *Bungo Manual: Selected Reference Materials for Students of Classical Japanese*

49 Susan Blakeley Klein, *Ankoku Butō: The Premodern and Postmodern Influences on the Dance of Utter Darkness*

50 Karen Brazell, ed., *Twelve Plays of the Noh and Kyōgen Theaters*

51 David G. Goodman, ed., *Five Plays by Kishida Kunio*

52 Shirō Hara, *Ode to Stone,* tr. James Morita

53 Peter J. Katzenstein & Yutaka Tsujinaka, *Defending the Japanese State: Structures, Norms and the Political Responses to Terrorism and Violent Social Protest in the 1970s and 1980s*

54 Su Xiaokang & Wang Luxiang, *Deathsong of the River: A Reader's Guide to the Chinese TV Series* Heshang, trs. Richard Bodman & Pin P. Wan

55 Jingyuan Zhang, *Psychoanalysis in China: Literary Transformations, 1919-1949*

56 Jane Kate Leonard & John R. Watt, eds., *To Achieve Security and Wealth: The Qing Imperial State and the Economy, 1644-1911*

57 Andrew F. Jones, *Like a Knife: Ideology and Genre in Contemporary Chinese Popular Music*

58 Peter J. Katzenstein & Nobuo Okawara, *Japan's National Security: Structures, Norms and Policy Responses in a Changing World*

59 Carsen Holz, *The Role of Central Banking in China's Economic Reforms*

60 Chifumi Shimazaki, *Warrior Ghost Plays from the Japanese Noh Theater: Parallel Translations with Running Commentary*

61 Emily Groszos Ooms, *Women and Millenarian Protest in Meiji Japan: Deguchi Nao and Ōmotokyō*

62 Carolyn Anne Morley, *Transformation, Miracles, and Mischief: The Mountain Priest Plays of Kyōgen*

63 David R. McCann & Hyunjae Yee Sallee, tr., *Selected Poems of Kim Namjo*, afterword by Kim Yunsik

64 HUA Qingzhao, *From Yalta to Panmunjom: Truman's Diplomacy and the Four Powers, 1945-1953*

65 Margaret Benton Fukasawa, *Kitahara Hakushū: His Life and Poetry*

66 Kam Louie, ed., *Strange Tales from Strange Lands: Stories by Zheng Wanlong*, with introduction

67 Wang Wen-hsing, *Backed Against the Sea*, tr. Edward Gunn

68 Brother Anthony of Taizé & Young-Moo Kim, trs., *The Sound of My Waves: Selected Poems by Ko Un*

69 Brian Myers, *Han Sŏrya and North Korean Literature: The Failure of Socialist Realism in the DPRK*

70 Thomas P. Lyons & Victor Nee, eds., *The Economic Transformation of South China: Reform and Development in the Post-Mao Era*

71 David G. Goodman, tr., *After Apocalypse: Four Japanese Plays of Hiroshima and Nagasaki*, with introduction

72 Thomas P. Lyons, *Poverty and Growth in a South China County: Anxi, Fujian, 1949-1992*

74 Martyn Atkins, *Informal Empire in Crisis: British Diplomacy and the Chinese Customs Succession, 1927-1929*

76 Chifumi Shimazaki, *Restless Spirits from Japanese Noh Plays of the Fourth Group: Parallel Translations with Running Commentary*

77 Brother Anthony of Taizé & Young-Moo Kim, trs., *Back to Heaven: Selected Poems of Ch'ŏn Sang Pyŏng*

78 Kevin O'Rourke, tr., *Singing Like a Cricket, Hooting Like an Owl: Selected Poems by Yi Kyu-bo*

79 Irit Averbuch, *The Gods Come Dancing: A Study of the Japanese Ritual Dance of Yamabushi Kagura*

80 Mark Peterson, *Korean Adoption and Inheritance: Case Studies in the Creation of a Classic Confucian Society*

81 Yenna Wu, tr., *The Lioness Roars: Shrew Stories from Late Imperial China*

82 Thomas Lyons, *The Economic Geography of Fujian: A Sourcebook*, Vol. 1

83 Pak Wan-so, *The Naked Tree*, tr. Yu Young-nan

84 C.T. Hsia, *The Classic Chinese Novel: A Critical Introduction*

85 Cho Chong-Rae, *Playing With Fire*, tr. Chun Kyung-Ja

86 Hayashi Fumiko, *I Saw a Pale Horse and Selections from Diary of a Vagabond*, tr. Janice Brown

87 Motoori Norinaga, *Kojiki-den, Book 1*, tr. Ann Wehmeyer

88 *Sending the Ship Out to the Stars: Poems of Park Je-chun,* tr. Chang Soo Ko

89 Thomas Lyons, *The Economic Geography of Fujian: A Sourcebook,* Vol. 2

90 Brother Anthony of Taizé, tr., *Midang: Early Lyrics of So Chong-Ju*

91 Chifumi Shimazaki, *Battle Noh: Parallel Translations with Running Commentary*

92 Janice Matsumura, *More Than a Momentary Nightmare: The Yokohama Incident and Wartime Japan*

93 Kim Jong-Gil, tr., *The Snow Falling on Chagall's Village: Selected Poems of Kim Ch'un-Su*

94 Wolhee Choe & Peter Fusco, trs., *Day-Shine: Poetry by Hyon-jong Chong*

95 Chifumi Shimazaki, *Troubled Souls from Japanese Noh Plays of the Fourth Group*

96 Hagiwara Sakutarō, *Principles of Poetry* (Shi no Genri), tr. Chester Wang

97 Mae J. Smethurst, *Dramatic Representations of Filial Piety: Five Noh in Translation*

98 Ross King, ed., *Description and Explanation in Korean Linguistics*

99 William Wilson, Hōgen Monogatari: *Tale of the Disorder in Hōgen*

100 Yasushi Yamanouchi, J. Victor Koschmann and Ryūichi Narita, eds., *Total War and 'Modernization'*

101 Yi Ch'ŏng-jun, *The Prophet and Other Stories,* tr. Julie Pickering

102 S.A. Thornton, *Charisma and Community Formation in Medieval Japan: The Case of the* Yugyō-ha *(1300-1700)*

103 Sherman Cochran, ed., *Inventing Nanjing Road: Commercial Culture in Shanghai, 1900-1945*

104 Harold M. Tanner, *Strike Hard! Anti-Crime Campaigns and Chinese Criminal Justice, 1979-1985*

105 Brother Anthony of Taizé & Young-Moo Kim, trs., *Farmers' Dance: Poems by Shin Kyong-nim*

106 Susan Orpett Long, ed., *Lives in Motion: Composing Circles of Self and Community in Japan*

107 Peter J. Katzenstein, Natasha Hamilton-Hart, Kozo Kato, & Ming Yue, *Asian Regionalism*

108 Kenneth Alan Grossberg, *Japan's Renaissance: the Politics of the Muromachi Bakufu*

109 John W. Hall & Toyoda Takeshi, eds., *Japan in the Muromachi Age*

110 Kim Su-Young, Shin Kyong-Nim, Lee Si-Young; *Variations: Three Korean Poets*; Brother Anthony of Taizé & Young-Moo Kim, trs.

111 Samuel Leiter, *Frozen Moments: Writings on* Kabuki, *1966-2001*

112 Pilwun Shih Wang & Sarah Wang, *Early One Spring: A Learning Guide to Accompany the Film Video* February

113 Thomas Conlan, *In Little Need of Divine Intervention: Scrolls of the Mongol Invasions of Japan*

114 Jane Kate Leonard & Robert Antony, eds., *Dragons, Tigers, and Dogs: Qing Crisis Management and the Boundaries of State Power in Late Imperial China*

115 Shu-ning Sciban & Fred Edwards, eds., *Dragonflies: Fiction by Chinese Women in the Twentieth Century*

116 David G. Goodman, ed., *The Return of the Gods: Japanese Drama and Culture in the 1960s*

117 Yang Hi Choe-Wall, *Vision of a Phoenix: The Poems of Hŏ Nansŏrhŏn*

118 Mae J. Smethurst, ed., *The Noh* Ominameshi: *A Flower Viewed from Many Directions*

119 Joseph A. Murphy, *Metaphorical Circuit: Negotiations Between Literature and Science in Twentieth-Century Japan*

FORTHCOMING

S. Yumiko Hulvey, *Sacred Rites in Moonlight: Ben no Naishi Nikki*

Charlotte von Verschuer, *Across the Perilous Sea: Japanese Trade with China and Korea from the 7ᵗʰ to the 16ᵗʰ Century*, Kristen Lee Hunter, tr.

Pang Kie-chung & Michael D. Shin, eds., *Landlords, Peasants, & Intellectuals in Modern Korea*

Fan Pen Chen, *Visions for the Masses: Chinese Shadow Plays from Shaanxi & Shanxi*

Ann Sung-hi Lee, *Yi Kwang-su, the Novel* Mujŏng, *and Modern Korean Literature*

Joan R. Piggott, ed., *Capital and Countryside in Japan, 300-1180: Japanese Historians Interpreted in English*

Brett de Bary, ed., *Deconstructing Nationality*

Kyoko Selden & Jolisa Gracewood, eds., *Modern Japanese Literature Readers*
Vol. 1 Stories by Tawada Yōko, Nakagami Kenji, and Hayashi Kyōko
Vol. 2 Stories by Natsume Sōseki, Inoue Yasushi, and Tomioka Taeko

Richard Calichman, *Takeuchi Yoshimi: Displacing the West*

Judith Rabinovitch and Timothy Bradstock, *Dance of the Butterflies:* Kanshi *(Chinese Poetry) from the Japanese Court Tradition*

Order online: www.einaudi.cornell.edu/eastasia/CEASbooks, or contact Cornell East Asia Series Distribution Center, 95 Brown Road, Box 1004, Ithaca, NY 14850, USA; toll-free: 1-877-865-2432, fax 607-255-7534, ceas@cornell.edu

www.ingramcontent.com/pod-product-compliance
Ingram Content Group UK Ltd.
Pitfield, Milton Keynes, MK11 3LW, UK
UKHW022033060225
454777UK00010B/810